THE SPEAKER'S BOOK
OF ILLUSTRATIONS

THE SPEAKER'S
BOOK OF
ILLUSTRATIONS

By HERBERT V. PROCHNOW

BAKER BOOK HOUSE
Grand Rapids, Michigan

Copyright © 1960 by
Baker Book House Company

ISBN: 0-8010-6920-3

Library of Congress Catalog Card Number: 60-15265

First printing, March, 1969
Second printing, March, 1972
Third printing, May, 1974

PHOTOLITHOPRINTED BY CUSHING - MALLOY, INC.
ANN ARBOR, MICHIGAN, UNITED STATES OF AMERICA
1974

PREFACE

This reference book, with its hundreds of items, is meant to be useful to many different groups of persons. There are epigrams, literary quotations, anecdotes from biography, humorous stories, inspiring illustrations, quotations from sermons and speeches, worthwhile thoughts of distinguished persons and many interesting facts and ideas.

The hundreds of items in the book will be helpful to those who serve occasionally or frequently as toastmaster or chairman of a meeting or who make speeches or deliver sermons. These items may be used in introductions or speeches to illustrate a point, to add humor or to provide inspiration.

Many of these illustrations may also be used by those who would like to enliven conversation and make it more interesting. In addition, they may be helpful in general discussions and informal meetings in presenting ideas in a colorful and effective manner.

Here is material that may constitute a source book for repeated use over the years.

HERBERT V. PROCHNOW

Evanston, Illinois

CONTENTS

CHAPTER I

WHEN YOU PRESIDE AND
WHEN YOU SPEAK

Many of us are so occupied with our daily responsibilities that we find it difficult to take the time to read at length regarding the responsibilities we occasionally assume as chairman or speaker. However, there are responsibilities associated with these assignments which we ought clearly to understand. To be helpful and to conserve the reader's time, there are outlined in this chapter some of your principal responsibilities when you preside and when you speak.

WHEN YOU PRESIDE

1. A successful meeting requires the greatest care and thoughtfulness in the selection of a speaker. You have nothing to gain and everything to lose by presiding at a meeting which the audience does not find worthwhile.

2. All arrangements such as publicity, the physical comfort of the audience, including proper ventilation and the proper reception of the speaker, should have been made in advance.

3. You will profit by having a carefully worked out time schedule for the meeting and by adhering to it. The speaker should have been informed regarding the time allotted for his remarks and should be given his full time.

4. Announcements during the meeting should be held to an absolute minimum, both as to number and length. Few things can be more boring than numerous long announcements.

5. If you have a seating arrangement for guests, be sure they are informed regarding the places assigned to them. The principal guest should be at the presiding officer's right.

6. As chairman, you should have your remarks carefully prepared in advance. Your comments should also be limited to the prepared time schedule.

7. The chairman should give the speaker a good introduc-

tion but not one so lavish that the speaker cannot possibly live up to it. The speaker and not the chairman should make the speech.

8. The speaker for any occasion should be carefully chosen for his ability to discharge the assignment well—and for no other reason. When he completes his address, he deserves a sincere expression of appreciation. If there is no honorarium, many groups nevertheless give the speaker at least a modest gift as a token of appreciation for his speech.

9. If the meeting permits, a light touch of humor in your comments as chairman will be welcome.

10. You have the full responsibility for conducting a meeting which is rewarding to those who attend it.

WHEN YOU SPEAK

1. One should never agree to make a speech without time for adequate preparation. There is no excuse for wasting the time of an audience.

2. In order to prepare an effective speech one obviously ought to have clearly in mind the exact subject to be discussed.

3. As a rule, it is better for a speaker to divide the body of the speech into two, three or four parts. This procedure requires a speaker to analyze his subject carefully in order to select the most important points for emphasis.

4. Use illustrations, facts and figures which interest and inform the listener. Vague generalities and abstractions are no substitute for definite and precise ideas.

5. There is no adequate substitute for knowledge of one's subject. Enthusiasm is a valuable quality in speaking, and enthusiasm is impossible without knowledge. No one can enthuse about nothing. A person who does not know his subject has nothing about which to enthuse.

6. An effective speech becomes more convincing as it proceeds until it reaches a climax.

7. In closing it is often helpful to outline the major points of the speech or to summarize the entire speech in a few words.

8. After the first draft of a speech is ready, it should be carefully revised and refined. All unnecessary words should be eliminated. Every idea must be clearly expressed.

9. In the final revision a suitable epigram or pertinent story may be included at appropriate intervals to stress a point. Stories, epigrams and illustrations should not be used unless they relate directly to the speech.

10. Finally, a speaker must never forget that he is taking the time of twenty-five, fifty, one hundred or five hundred people for perhaps thirty minutes. It is his responsibility to make this time worthwhile.

CHAPTER II

EPIGRAMS AND QUIPS

Success would be a little more attractive if successful men seemed happier.

Enough money means more money than you now have.

You can be on the right track and still get run over if you are standing still.

The clothes that make a woman break a man.

Most of us have sufficient courage to stand the other fellow's hard luck.

The average woman wants a strong man she can wind around her finger.

The fellow who believes no two people think alike will change his mind when he gets married and looks over the wedding gifts.

The road of the automobile transgressor is hard surfaced.

One headlight is enough if the other driver guesses correctly which side it is on.

It is very difficult to like a person with whom you can't find any fault.

One thing about paying high taxes is that it does away with the need for a will.   *Herbert V. Prochnow*

Why criticise a person for talking about himself when that may be the only subject about which he is least uninformed.

We have seen pictures of college students engaged in various sports, but we've never seen a picture of one taking home a book from the library.

Money talks and most of us never get bored listening.

We like the fellow who comes right out and says he agrees with us.

In the old days we had one Death Valley, but now we have one between the curbs in every city.

Common sense would avoid many divorces and also quite a few marriages.

When you find that famous people are just like you are, it tends to make you feel very humble.

In the old days a woman's face was her fortune, but now it's the beauty parlor's.

We suppose the financial success of some novels and plays these days might be called striking pay dirt.

On juvenile delinquency we would say with the poet, "Oh, for the smack of a vanished hand on the place where the spank ought to be."

In the old days you opened the door and listened to a peddler, but now you sit down and turn on the television.

Herbert V. Prochnow

We have only a few illiterates in the United States, but millions of persons who can't read traffic signs.

The voice that father gets in Christmas shopping is the invoice.

A woman's idea of keeping a secret is to tell it to only one person at a time.

Many politicians are for and against an issue and they don't care who knows it.

It would be wonderful to be so well to do that the Joneses would try to keep up with you.

Always borrow from a pessimist. He never expects to be repaid.

It's easy to die with your boots on, if they're on the accelerator.

An optimist is a person who saves the pictures in the seed catalog to compare them with the flowers and vegetables he grows.

A patriot is a person who saves enough of his salary each week to pay his income tax.

Not only are the sins of the fathers visited upon the children, but now-a-days the sins of the children are visited upon the fathers.

The man who says he's a 100 per cent American probably made the appraisal himself.   *Herbert V. Prochnow*

An honest city is one where no one knows a rich policeman.

A pedagog works against ignorance, but a demagog gets a profit out of it.

It's no disgrace to be poor and, besides, the instalment salesmen leave you alone.

When we hear some popular songs, we are sure the illiteracy rate is still pretty high.

There may be songs that never die, but it isn't the fault of TV or radio.

A monologue is a conversation between a traffic cop and an automobile driver.

If the average husband bought a house costing twice his income, he would get either a wigwam or an igloo.

If all the toastmasters in the world were placed end to end, the silence would be very restful.

The fellow who argues that all religions should unite probably doesn't speak to his brother-in-law.

The bumptious guy usually gets bumped.

The fellow who does nothing is doing somebody.

If a buttercup is yellow, is a hiccup burple?
                                        Herbert V. Prochnow

You can lead high school graduates to college, but you cannot make them think.

It is not only a man's sins, but his creditors who find him out.

Frenchmen have a sense of humor, as every tourist finds when he tries to talk to them in French.

A politician will consider every way of reducing taxes except cutting expenses.

An intellectual is a person who is so smart that he can't understand the obvious.

A secret is what you ask someone else not to tell because you can't keep it.

The mosquito that buzzes the loudest gets swatted first.

Progress—In the old days a girl got her good looks from her mother. Now she gets them from the beauty parlor.

A man finds it about as hard to thread a needle as a woman does to drive through a twelve foot garage door.

Some persons diet on any kind of food they can get.

An idea may be dressed in attractive words and still be stupid.

If we get pay television, we suppose they will pay us for listening to some programs.   *Herbert V. Prochnow*

When you sow wild oats, you always get a bumper crop.

Early to bed and early to rise and you will keep out of the way of the boss.

Well-dressed ignorance often goes a long way.

It is very difficult for some persons to keep quiet when they have nothing to say.

Fortunately most popular songs decompose shortly after they are composed.

You can't help but admire the fellow who is stupid, but knows it.

The modern girl's hair may look like a mop, but she doesn't know what a mop looks like.

Money may make the mare go, but it's instalment credit that runs cars.

No garden is a failure if your neighbor's chickens take first prize at the poultry show.

Maybe more youngsters would stay home nights if they weren't afraid to stay alone in the house.

The remarkable thing about most of us is our ability to live beyond our means.

You can do a lot of good in the world if you don't care who gets credit for it.

Many people don't understand that "How are You" is a greeting and not a question.   *Herbert V. Prochnow*

Even a waiter sometimes comes to him who waits.

If it weren't for parking meters and the church collection plates, the government could do away with nickels.

A polite person never yawns and another polite person never notices it when he does.

One reason it's better to breathe through your nose is that it keeps your mouth shut.

The Lord provides but not necessarily in the style to which you might like to be accustomed.

The person who takes the worst view of things is probably a candid camera fan.

There is very little difference between men, but that little is enough.

The trouble with the world is that there are too many clowns who aren't in the circus.

It's always good fishing before you get there and after you leave.

It doesn't pay to brood—only the chickens get paid for it.

An argument is when two people try to get the last word in first.

The reason talk is cheap is that the supply always exceeds the demand.

As you grow older, you grow wiser, talk less, but say more.
Herbert V. Prochnow

If you are losing in an argument with your wife, tell her how wonderful she is.

You can fool all the people some of the time, but you can fool yourself all the time.

Whenever a person gets too big to study, he is as big as he will ever be.

If we learn by doing things, a lot of people are going to keep on being ignorant.

It's easier to make ends meet without too many easy payment plans.

No one becomes wise who is sure he already is.

Flattery is telling the other person what he thinks of himself.

All things come to the other fellow if you sit down and wait.

Fifty years ago a man who drove 25 miles an hour in an automobile was a sensation and he would be today also.

The wonderful thing about a dull party is that you can get home early.

There is a great deal of difference in thinking of yourself and thinking for yourself. *Herbert V. Prochnow*

If both sides of an argument make you laugh, you are either stupid or broad-minded.

The one thing you learn from experience is that you can't make money without working.

If a married couple never quarrel, they miss all the fun of making up.

A secret is either not worth keeping or it's too good to keep.

A yawn is poor manners, but it tells the speaker how you feel about his speech.

Confucius say: No man who catches large fish goes home through alley.

When you smoke in bed, the ashes that fall on the floor may be your own.

Education is what parents get when the children are home from school on vacation.

Sometimes we long for the good old days when we were young and knew everything.

One look at the dents in your fenders makes you realize this is a machine age.

No one writes fiction as well as the weather man.

One way to get along in life is to cooperate with the inevitable.　　　　　　　　　　　　　　*Herbert V. Prochnow*

Many a family argument has been saved by the doorbell or telephone.

You never feel more like a miserable failure than when your new car goes dead in traffic.

The person who agrees with you completely is probably not worth talking to.

Machines are almost human now because they can do things without using intelligence.

Sometimes you wonder just why anyone should feel superior to anyone else.

A Texas fisherman said the fish he caught was too small to bother with, so he got two men to help him throw it back into the water.

Most of us could pay as we go if we didn't go so much.

The best known popular sport today is running into debt.

Some men marry for looks but not the kind they get when they come home late for dinner.

A husband looked at his house, his car and his furniture and said it was wonderful so many people made a living on what he had not paid for. *Herbert V. Prochnow*

You get out of a mirror what you put in it and out of a scale what you put on it.

When we think of all the lonely people who have no friends, relatives or neighbors, we sort of envy them.

Women today expect their husbands to bring home the bacon, but only after the delicatessen has fried it.

We like the fellow who is reasonable and does things our way.

Sometimes a go-getter is sorry he gotter.

It's easy to pick out the best people because they'll help you do it.

There are more than 200,000 useless words in the English language and at some committee meetings you hear all of them.

A road hog and reckless driver is any other motorist.

An efficient business man who found a machine that would do half his work at the office bought two.

One reason you can't take it with you is that you don't have any left when you go.

It may be bad to talk when your mouth is full, but it isn't too good either when your head is empty.

It always pays to smile in the morning, because later in the day you may not feel like it. *Herbert V. Prochnow*

Too often when conscience tries to speak the line seems to be busy.

Nothing in the world is fool-proof as long as there is a fool.

If you are trying to kill time, always make sure it is your own.

A man's achievements in business depend partly on whether he keeps his mind or his feet on the desk.

No one has a touch that thrills you like a dentist.

A newspaper says it's dangerous for a young man to propose while he is driving a car. It's dangerous anywhere, son.

Before marriage he talks and she listens. After marriage she talks and he listens. Later they both talk and the neighbors listen.

We may not get a radio message as high as Mars, but they should be able to see our consumer price index.

It takes a conscientious politician to take nothing from the pie counter but his elbows.

Nowadays we spend so much on luxuries we can't afford the necessities.

A pessimist is a person who is happy when he is wrong.

Nothing sells as well as experience. Everyone is constantly buying it.   *Herbert V. Prochnow*

If you want to live to see 90, don't look for it on the speedometer.

If ignorance is bliss, an intelligence test is certainly a waste of time.

The average income figures of doctors indicate that the surgeon doesn't get as big a cut as you think.

We've heard some radio sopranos who must work only for the love of mike.

Nothing in life is as serious as a hotel waiter in a dinner jacket makes it.

In the old days children were necessities and automobiles luxuries. Now they're reversed.

Honesty is still the best policy, but some persons are satisfied with less than the best.

When you spend an evening at home, you never have to pay a quarter to get your hat back.

When a successful person lets his success go to his head, it often ends in defeat.

Some people are not only pleasure bent but pleasure broke.

If you feel that you have no faults, that makes another one.
Herbert V. Prochnow

When you make money gradually worth less, it may end being worthless.

If a wife wants to know how business is, all she has to do is ask her husband for a mink coat.

A scientist says even pure-looking air has dirt suspended in it. He apparently has a radio and television.

When some people say, "Get thee behind me Satan," they're inviting him to get behind and push.

A tenant has about as hard a time collecting the rent as the landlord does.

A dollar doesn't go as far as it used to, but it's just as hard to get back.

Any month that doesn't have a "Q" in its spelling is free from income tax worries.

The thing we don't like about Father Time is that he doesn't sell round trips.

We suppose this country could be so well protected against cheap foreign labor that the foreign labor couldn't even buy high-priced American goods.

Few politicians die because of ideals, but a great many ideals die because of politicians. *Herbert V. Prochnow*

Money talks, but the folks who know how to save it don't.

In the old days history was made for a tenth of what it costs today.

The first world was made out of chaos and the same materials are ready now.

A platitude is a wise crack you have heard before.

Today a dollar earned is a nickel saved.

To be tactful is to let someone else do something you want done.

In world affairs nothing sounds so ominous as the rumbling of empty stomachs.

The high school senior said a deacon is what you place on top of a skyscraper to guide airplanes.

The thing we don't like about farming is that soil rhymes with toil.

First, men fight for freedom, and then they make laws gradually to take it away.

Sometimes we think the world is made of buffer states and bluffer states.

Progress: In the old days the owners were under the cars. Now the pedestrians are.

One person you have to watch if you are going to save money is yourself.   *Herbert V. Prochnow*

Education helps you to earn more. But not many school teachers can prove it.

To have average intelligence is to be less stupid than half of the people and more stupid than the other half.

Today, if one man can do a job in one hour, four men can do it in four hours.

The person who closes his mouth before someone else wants him to has passed one of the tests for success.

Evening is the time of day when people do anything to keep from going to bed and getting eight hours sleep.

Some people won't take it with them because they didn't save any to take.

The man who boasts that he never made a mistake has a wife who did.

He who hesitates misses the green light, gets bumped in the rear and loses his parking place.

A punctual person is patient, because he gets that way waiting for those who are not punctual.

If you have some hard bumps, you are probably traveling out of the rut.

A good many people can make a speech, but saying something is more difficult.   *Herbert V. Prochnow*

Money doesn't make fools of persons, but it does tend to show them up.

Most of us find that it's hard to take advice from people who need it worse than we do.

When a person really knows himself, he probably wonders why he has so many friends.

Most of us would prefer to be miserably rich than happily poor.

To entertain some people all you have to do is sit and listen.

A good wife always helps her husband with the housework.

Ten years from now we'll laugh at the clothes women wear today, but can we hold in that long.

It's hard to suffer in silence, because that takes all the pleasure out of the suffering.

Nature abhors a vacuum and she sometimes fills an empty head with conceit.

About all the world sees of the peace dove is the bill.

With a high standard of living people are often better off than they are better.

A boy is grown up when he walks around a puddle.

Herbert V. Prochnow

It annoys a woman to have her friends drop in and find the house looking as it usually does.

If you can make your guests feel at home when you wish they were, you are a good host.

When a fat man laughs, a great deal of him has a good time.

Remember, your relatives had no choice in the matter either.

No married man can understand what a bachelor does with his money.

It isn't easy for an idea to squeeze into a head filled with prejudices.

As the sweet young thing said when she took a golf lesson, "Now which club do I use for a hole-in-one."

Your income is the amount of money no matter how much you get you spend more than.

No one knows how to save money as well as the person who hasn't any.

By the time a woman is married five years she knows how to slight the housework where it doesn't show.

Our homes are being filled with gadgets that are smarter than we are and cost more to repair.

Hard work is an accumulation of easy things you should have done earlier.   *Herbert V. Prochnow*

What the present generation needs is a tabloid Bible.

Most moving pictures are more to be pitied than censored.

With apologies to Benjamin Franklin: "Early to bed and early to rise—with present taxes you can't earn enough to do otherwise."

Father's business may not be good, but mother's is always picking up.

There is only a little difference between sticking your neck out and keeping your chin up, but that difference is important.

When day is done and evening falls, you often find nothing else is done.

Conscience is the still small voice that makes you feel even smaller.

The worst thing about winter nights is that by the time your feet get warm you've overslept.

Car sickness is the feeling some persons get when each month's installment comes due.

It's always annoying to have two people talk while we're interrupting.

In the old days a delinquent was a youngster who owed a few cents on an overdue library book.

All men are born equal, but what they are equal to is the important thing.   *Herbert V. Prochnow*

A person can win a lot of arguments by avoiding them.

No one has more faith than the person who plays a slot machine.

Literary Critic: A person who will discuss the social objectives of a book that never had any.

As people get better off, they sometimes have too much to live on and too little to live for.

Half a loaf is better than no time off.

When you sing your own praise, you always get the tune too high.

Fortunately the future only comes one day at a time.

CHAPTER III

ANECDOTES AND QUOTATIONS
FROM BIOGRAPHY

TACT

Alexandre Dumas, the French novelist, was once stopped in Paris by a beggar who asked for alms in a rather threatening manner. Said Dumas: "Why do you not take off your hat to me when you ask for money?"

"Honorable sir," replied the man, "over on the corner stands a policeman. If he sees me take off my hat he will know that I am begging and will at once arrest me. As it is, he thinks that we are merely two old acquaintances having a chat."

Dumas was so impressed by the man's ready retort he gave him 100 francs.   *Tit-Bits, London*

YOU LOSE

When President Coolidge was president, his fame as a man of few words had spread far and wide, even to a dinner party in a New England town to which he was invited. At the party, two women made a bet. When Mr. Coolidge was seated, one of the women stepped up to him and confessed that she had put up $5 as a wager that she could make the President say at least three words in the first five minutes.

Mr. Coolidge turned to the woman, gave her a gracious smile, and said, "You lose."

HIS IDEAL

Some years ago there was a boy in England who was facing a great future, in spite of the fact that his grades were not always what they should have been.

That boy had an ideal. He had a passionate admiration for his father, who stood high in English public life. This lad once said, "The thing I want most to be is to be as honest and fearless as my father."

He had his wish. His name was Winston Churchill.

NOT THE WORD

Franz Liszt, no less a diplomat than a musician, had a stock reply for young women, particularly pretty ones, who demanded unmerited praise of their singing.

"Maestro," a young thing would inquire, "do you not think I have a good voice?"

"Ah, my dear young lady," Liszt would reply with vibrant sincerity, " 'good' is not the word."

PRESENTING

At a recent meeting the chairman introduced Bob Hope with these lines: "I want to present the funniest comedian in pictures, one of the screen's handsomest leading men, and the fellow who generously wrote this introduction for me—Bob Hope!"

THE JOY OF APPRECIATION

As a simple, unpretentious admirer of fine art, Elbert Hubbard derived much pleasure from visiting the great art galleries. One day he was admiring a priceless painting in a New York gallery when a friend chidingly remarked, "Elbert, why do you allow yourself to become so enthused over things you can never afford to own?"

"Harry," replied the sage of East Aurora, "I would rather be able to appreciate things I cannot have than to have things I am not able to appreciate."   *Christian Science Monitor*

COMMENTS OF FRANKLIN P. ADAMS

Accustomed as I am to public speaking, I know the futility of it.

The best part of the fiction in many novels is the notice that the characters are all purely imaginary.

Count that day won when, turning on its axis, this earth imposes no additional taxes.

You never know what you can do without until you try.

IN SCHOOL, NO APPLES, NO NOTHIN'

The teacher was trying to impress on the children how important had been the discovery of the law of gravitation.

"Sir Isaac Newton was sitting on the ground, looking at the tree," she said. "An apple fell on his head, and from that he discovered gravitation. Just think, children," she added enthusiastically, "isn't that wonderful?"

The inevitable small boy replied, "Yes'm; an' if he had been settin' in school lookin' at his books, he wouldn't never have discovered nothin'!"

JUST A NOVELTY!

Frank B. Woods was one of those present when the Wright brothers made their historic flights at Kitty Hawk, N. C., on December 17, 1903. Mr. Woods recalled that occasion in these words: "I rode down with Barney Oldfield. It was a bitter cold day with a high wind. We stood around awhile watching the boys. Then I went back to the Coast Guard station to get warm, and missed the third flight. Barney and I agreed that the airplane was a novelty, but would never amount to anything."

WHAT A BUG!

Charles Robert Darwin, the great scientist, was invited one day to a friend's house. Soon after his arrival, two small boys rushed into the room and asked Mr. Darwin if he could tell them the name of the creature they held in their hands.

Now, the "creature" was one they had carefully put together to fool Mr. Darwin. They had stuck the wings of a dead bluebottle fly into the body of a butterfly, and added parts of a grasshopper, daddy longlegs, and a black beetle.

Mr. Darwin eyed the thing, and looked at the boys. "Did the creature hum very much when you caught it?" he asked solemnly.

"Why—yes—I think it hummed," answered one of the boys.

"Are you quite sure?" asked Mr. Darwin.

"Why—yes—I think I'm quite sure," said the boy.

"Then," replied the great scientist, "it's a humbug."

NO BRIEF CANDLE

Life is no brief candle to me. It is a sort of splendid torch which I have got hold of for the moment, and I want to make it burn as brightly as possible before handing it on to future generations.   *George Bernard Shaw*

HARDSHIP

Thomas Edison lost most of his hearing at about eight years of age, but he gave us the electric light, phonograph, movies, and over a hundred other useful inventions.

There was another man who had terrible hemorrhages of the lungs, and he almost died several times from coughing spells. Yet, while he was an invalid, he gave us at least two masterpieces, *Treasure Island* and *Dr. Jekyll and Mr. Hyde.* He was Robert Louis Stevenson.

There was a young man who was ill and unhappy most of his short life—heart trouble at seventeen, inherited physical weaknesses, an orphan before he was three and taken in by strangers, kicked out of school, suffered from poverty, and had no fame until after his pitiful death at the young age of forty. Yet, in the short space of about twenty years, he gave the world—articles, essays, brilliant criticisms. His poetry is widely read. He wrote short stories and detective stories, and one of his poems is on exhibit at the world-famous Huntington Library, at San Marino, California, and is worth $50,000. This poor young invalid was a great literary genius, Edgar Allan Poe.

COOL $22 MILLION

Not every revolutionary idea comes from professional inventors.

Many of the big ideas come to fruition because someone was alert enough to build upon an accident.

Ice cream was the result of some accidental frozen custard.

Other ideas, too, like the one of the U. S. naturalist who was doing research in Labrador and noticed that meat frozen in 40 below weather tasted a lot better than meat frozen more slowly.

Back home, he tried quick-freezing a variety of foods and started a frozen food business. His name: Clarence Birdseye. He sold the business in 1929 for $22,000,000.

The Postage Stamp

QUIET

Arturo Toscanini, the great symphony conductor who recently retired, says this is one of his favorite stories. An orchestra was playing Beethoven's Leonore overture, the two climaxes of which are each followed by a trumpet passage offstage.

The first climax arrived, but not a sound came from the trumpet. The conductor, annoyed, went on to the second climax. Again—no trumpet.

This time, the conductor rushed into the wings. There he found the trumpet player struggling with the house fireman.

"I tell you, you can't play that trumpet back here!" the fireman was insisting. "There's a concert going on!"

REMINDER

Paderewski appreciated fine food. After a dinner at his favorite restaurant, he told the waiter, "The fish was excellent, the meat delicious, and the dessert very good." The waiter went to the kitchen, but soon came back and said to Paderewski, "The chef wishes to thank you, sir, and wants me to tell you that the soup was good, too."   *Nicolas Slonimsky, Etude*

HIS MOST IMPORTANT THOUGHT

A friend once put to Daniel Webster this question, "Mr. Webster, what do you consider the most important thought that ever occupied your mind?" And immediately the great statesman flashed back, "The most important thought that has ever occupied my mind was that of my individual responsibility to God."   *Harold W. Ruopp, Christian Advocate*

"I LIKE TO WORK"

Booker T. Washington, according to *The Penn-Trail,* shortly after he had taken charge of the Tuskegee Institute in Alabama, passed the house of a wealthy family. The woman of the house, not knowing Mr. Washington by sight, asked if he would chop some wood.

Professor Washington took off his coat and chopped the wood. He also carried it into the kitchen. There a servant girl recognized him, and later told her mistress of his identity.

The next morning the woman went to Professor Washington's office and apologized, saying, "I did not know it was you I put to work."

"It's entirely all right, madam," the great Negro replied; "I like to work, and I'm delighted to do favors for my friends."

His simple act won this woman's admiration, and she persuaded wealthy acquaintances to give thousands of dollars to the school.   *Sunshine Magazine*

BLURRED VISION

According to Liehtze, the Chinese philosopher, there was once a man in the Kingdom of Ch'i who craved gold. He went to a shop that sold gold, grabbed some and ran. The police arrested him and asked, "How could you rob somebody else's gold in broad daylight and in front of all those people, too?"

The man of Ch'i answered, "When I reached for the gold, I saw only gold. I didn't see any people."

Property, Cambridge Associates

JEFFERSON'S GREAT OPPORTUNITY

After the Continental Congress had long debated the subject of independence, it appointed a committee, consisting of Benjamin Franklin, John Adams, Robert Livingston, and Thomas Jefferson, to draw up a declaration to which they might affix their names. Four days before, Richard Henry Lee had offered this resolution: "That the united colonies are, and of right ought to be, free and independent states; that they are absolved from all allegiance to the British Crown, and that all political connection between them and the state of Great Britain is, and ought to be, totally dissolved."

On the day before the appointment of the committee to write the declaration, Mr. Lee was called home by the illness of his wife. Had it not been for this, doubtless he would have been made chairman of the committee, and would perhaps have written the declaration. As matters were, Thomas Jefferson, the youngest member of the committee, was asked to write the document. Adams and Franklin made a few alterations in the paper as Mr. Jefferson wrote it, and thus there came into being what is considered one of the most important papers written by the pen of man.

Jefferson had been appointed as a member of the Congress only a short time before, to fill a vacancy caused by a resignation. He remained a member only a few months. But Jefferson was ready for his opportunity.

DEBT TO OTHERS

A hundred times every day I remind myself that my inner and outer life depend on the labors of other men, living and dead, and that I must exert myself in order to give in the same measure as I have received and am still receiving.

Albert Einstein

WELLINGTON AND NAPOLEON

The Duke of Wellington and Napoleon Bonaparte were both born in the same year, 1769. Each was born on an island, each became fatherless in early boyhood, each had four brothers and three sisters, each attended military school in France and at the same time. Both became lieutenant-colonels within a day of each other, both excelled at mathematics, both were great soldiers, and each commanded a great army. And both are remembered for what happened at Waterloo, where one became the victor and the other the vanquished!

WRONG GUESSES

A Boston newspaper some seventy-three years ago reported: "Joshua Coppersmith has been arrested for trying to extort funds from ignorant and superstitious people by a device which he says will convey the human voice over wires. He calls the instrument a telephone."

In a book published in 1933, Dorothy Thompson related that it took her just 50 seconds after meeting Adolf Hitler to decide that "that formless, almost faceless man" would never become the dictator of Germany.

Here's how the Chicago Times in 1865 evaluated Lincoln's Gettysburg Address in commenting on it the day after its delivery: "The cheek of every American must tingle with shame as he reads the silly, flat, and dish-watery utterances of a man who has to be pointed out to intelligent foreigners as President of the United States."

In many a public speech, the great Daniel Webster expressed his doubt concerning the ultimate success of American railroads. He argued that frost on the rails would prevent a train from moving; or, if it did move, it could not be brought to a stop.

And most people who loaned money to Robert Fulton for the development of his proposed steamboat did so with the stipulation that their names be kept secret, for fear they might be ridiculed for backing such an absurd idea.

Adapted from Youth Today

REMARKS OF ROBERT BENCHLEY

Drawing on my fine command of language, I said nothing.

In America there are two classes of travel—first class, and with children.

It took me fifteen years to discover I had no talent for writing, but I couldn't give it up because by that time I was too famous.

It was one of those plays in which all the actors unfortunately enunciated very clearly.

PERFECTION

In the British Museum one can see 75 drafts of Thomas Gray's poem, "Elegy Written in a Country Churchyard." Gray didn't like the first way he wrote it, nor the second nor the third. He wasn't satisfied till he scribbled it over and over 75 times.   *Household Magazine*

THE EDISON SPONGE

Thomas A. Edison, the great inventor, was talking one day with the governor of North Carolina, and the governor complimented him on his inventive genius.

"I am not a great inventor," said Edison.

"But you have over a thousand patents to your credit, haven't you?" queried the governor.

"Yes, but about the only invention I can really claim as absolutely original is the phonograph," was the reply.

"Why, I'm afraid I don't understand what you mean," said the governor.

"Well," explained Edison, "I guess I'm an awfully good sponge. I absorb ideas from every source I can, and put them to practical use. Then I improve them until they become of some value. The ideas which I use are mostly the ideas of other people who don't develop them themselves."

Adapted from Just a Moment

STOOP

I like to remember the story Benjamin Franklin used to tell about the return visit he made to Boston when he was twenty-one. He went for advice to Cotton Mather, and this in Franklin's words is what happened, "He received me in his library and, on my taking leave, showed me a shorter way out of the house through a narrow passage, which was crossed by a beam overhead. We were still talking as I withdrew, he accompanying me behind, when he said hastily: 'Stoop, stoop!' I did not understand him, till I felt my head hit against the beam. He was a man that never missed any occasion of giving instruction, and upon this he said to me: 'You are young, and have the world before you; stoop as you go through it, and you will miss many hard bumps.'"   *Edward Weeks*

ABRAHAM LINCOLN

Among the million words in the Lincoln utterance record, he interprets himself with a more keen precision than someone else offering to explain him.

Infinitely tender was his word from a White House balcony to a crowd on the White House lawn:

> I have not willingly planted a thorn in any man's bosom.

Or to a military Governor:

> I shall do nothing through malice; what I deal with is too vast for malice.

He wrote for Congress to read on December 1, 1862:

> In times like the present, men should utter nothing for which they would not willingly be responsible through time and eternity.   *Carl Sandburg*

WHY?

Once at a Savoy luncheon in honor of John Mason Brown, James Agate took his own sly way of enhancing Anglo-American friendship:

"Tell me, Brown," he said, "why do you Americans, delightful individually, taken collectively add up to a nation of twerps?"

To which John Mason Brown, the Confederate Aristotle, magnificently replied:

"All right, Agate, why with you Britishers, is the converse the case?"

Orville Prescott, quoted by Dan Herr in Books on Trial

HE WOULDN'T QUIT

Engineers were called in to give their ideas on a possible railroad through the Andes Mountains. These men proclaimed the job as an impossible one. Then American engineers were called in to give their opinions whether the railroad could follow along the side of the River Rimac. Even these intrepid engineers claimed that it could not be done. As a last resort, a Polish engineer named Ernest Malinowski was called in. Malinowski's reputation as an engineer was well known, but he was at that time in his sixtieth year, so the authorities feared to impose such a rigorous task on the man.

Malinowski assured the representatives of the various countries interested that the job could be done, and in his sixtieth year he started the highest railroad in the world.

The railroad began to worm its way across the Andes from Peru with sixty-two tunnels and thirty bridges along its way. One tunnel ran 4,000 feet in length, 15,000 feet above the level of the sea. Twice, revolutions of some of the countries through which the railroad passed, held up construction. Once Malinowski had to flee Peru and remain in exile for a time—but nothing deterred this aging Pole in completing the engineering feat that became one of the wonders of the world in 1880.

Future

DEFINITIONS OF AMBROSE BIERCE

Acquaintance: a degree of friendship called slight when its object is poor or obscure, and intimate when he is rich or famous.

Admiration: our polite recognition of another man's resemblance to ourselves.

All are lunatics, but he who can analyze his delusion is called a philosopher.

Bore: a person who talks when you wish him to listen.

Calamities are of two kinds: misfortune to ourselves, and good fortune to others.

A conservative is a statesman who is enamored of existing evils, as distinguished from the liberal who wishes to replace them with others.

Coward: one who in a perilous emergency thinks with his legs.

Discussion: a method of confirming others in their errors.

Egotist: a person of low taste, more interested in himself than in me.

Experience is a revelation in the light of which we renounce our errors of youth for those of age.

Hospitality: the virtue which induces us to feed and lodge certain persons who are not in need of food and lodging.

Lecturer: one with his hand in your pocket, his tongue in your ear, and his faith in your patience.

Positive: being mistaken at the top of one's voice.

A prejudice is a vagrant opinion without visible means of support.

To apologize is to lay the foundation for a future offense.

To the small part of ignorance that we arrange and classify we give the name knowledge.

"MY BOSS WON'T LET ME"

One day, when one of his secretaries suggested dropping work for a diversion which he knew would appeal to Woodrow Wilson, the President replied, "My boss won't let me do it."

"Your boss?" questioned the friend, wondering who could be the boss of the chief executive of the United States.

"Yes, I have a conscience that is my boss," said the President. "It drives me to the task, and will not let me accept the tempting invitation."

A PRAYER

If I had my way—and I haven't—I would have inscribed over the door of the United Nations building the prayer of St. Francis of Assisi, "O Lord, make me an instrument of Thy peace." *Henry Cabot Lodge, Jr.*

GREATNESS IS BEFORE YOU

John Keats lived just twenty-six years, yet his poetry will live forever, much of it equal to that of Shakespeare. Franz Schubert died at thirty-one. In those thirty-one years he wrote more than 110 musical compositions, more than sixty of them lyric songs.

Here is a boy so ugly and ridiculously clothed that he was tormented by his schoolmates. He spent his time reading to forget his misery. At eighteen he worked as a bricklayer. But he finally won the acclaim and esteem of England. He was honored by Queen Elizabeth and decorated by King James.

His name was Ben Jonson, and he was one of the most brilliant playwrights England ever produced.

Here is a morbid, sensitive son of a poor preacher. He was regarded as a stupid blockhead in the village school. When he finally got a degree from college, he was the lowest on the list. He was rejected for the ministry. He tried law with the same result. He borrowed a suit of clothes to take an examination as a hospital mate, failed, and pawned his clothes. He lived in garrets, failing at everything he tried. Only one thing he wanted to do—write. This he did and rose above the handicaps of illness, poverty, and obscurity to high rank among the greatest writers of all time. His name was Oliver Goldsmith.

The world today is waiting for people out of step—men who dare think, men who refuse to be grasshoppers, men who dare stand on their own feet. The world said, "The earth is ruled by the mighty." But a young Galilean said, "Blessed are the meek: for they shall inherit the earth." He lived in an empire of power, possessions, and pleasure, but he said, "A man's life consisteth not in the abundance of the things which he possesseth." So they organized a mob and crucified him—a young man of thirty-three. What happened? Empires were lifted off their hinges. The course of human history was changed. New standards of life were established.

There are people who fail because they are afraid to make a beginning; who go to bed tired because they spend the day looking for an easy job; who cannot tell what they think about anything until they see what the morning paper has to say about it.   *George L. Rinliff in The Uplift*

OBSERVATIONS OF GILBERT CHESTERTON

The Bible tells us to love our neighbours, and also to love our enemies; probably because they are generally the same people.

Christianity has not been tried and found wanting; it has been found difficult and not tried.

The golden age only comes to men when they have, if only for a moment, forgotten gold.

I believe in getting into hot water; it keeps you clean.

I hate a quarrel because it interrupts an argument.

Optimism: the noble temptation to see too much in everything.

A puritan is a person who pours righteous indignation into the wrong things.

Silence is the unbearable repartee.

Yawn: a silent shout.

WHEN OBSTACLES CONFRONT US

The successful man lengthens his stride when he discovers that the signpost has deceived him; the failure looks for a place to sit down. Thomas Edison did not sit down and give up when his first efforts to find an effective filament for the carbon incandescent lamp met with failure. He lengthened his stride! He sent men to China, Japan, South America, Asia, Jamaica, Ceylon, and Burma in search of fibres and grasses to be tested in his laboratory.

Luther Burbank, the plant wizard, did not quit when obstacles blocked his way. At one time he personally conducted more than six thousand experiments before he found the solution.

George Westinghouse was treated as a mild lunatic by most railroad executives. "Stopping a train by wind! The man's crazy!" Yet he persevered, and finally sold the air-brake idea.

James Watt built model after model of his steam engine before he got one that worked efficiently.

Every man gets on the wrong road at times. He comes upon hills, rough roads, and dangerous detours. What he does when he meets these obstacles determines his destiny. The world never hears from those who look for a place to sit down and quit.

WISE DEDUCTION

The poet, Tasso, upon receiving reports from friends that a certain enemy was spreading gossip about him, observed:

"I am not disturbed. How much better it is that he speak ill of me to all the world than that all the world should speak ill of me to him."

TROUBLE

Whenever we start something new, and anybody comes to me and says, "Don't you think you are going to have a lot of trouble?" I say, "Sure, any time you start to do anything new, we will guarantee the trouble." Success depends on whether you get through the trouble or not.   *Charles F. Kettering*

VIEWPOINTS OF FINLEY PETER DUNNE (CREATOR OF MR. DOOLEY)

If a man is wise, he gets rich, and if he gets rich, he gets foolish, or his wife does.

A man never becomes an orator if he has anything to say.

The past always looks better than it was; it's only pleasant because it isn't here.

The wise people are in New York because the foolish went there first; that's the way the wise men make a living.

HOW IS MR. ADAMS?

A young woman once stopped John Quincy Adams on the street to ask, "And how is Mr. Adams today?" The elderly statesman was then ninety-one years of age. He replied somewhat like this, "Mr. Adams is very well, thank you. It is true that his house is falling apart. The foundations have settled, the rafters sag and the roof leaks a bit. He will be moving out almost any day now. But Mr. Adams is well, thank you, very well." Life had taught him, as it does all who grow up in faith, to believe in what lies beyond the rim of the visible.

GIVE

Let me say that no richer blessing can fill your own hearts than the consciousness on some bleak winter's night that your generosity has lighted the fire upon some family's hearth that otherwise would be black and cold, and has spread some family table with food where otherwise children would be wanting. I wish my last word to you to be the word "give."

Herbert Clark Hoover

MICHELANGELO WASN'T SATISFIED

There is no question about Michelangelo's secure position in the history of art. He stands head and shoulders above the sculptors of all time. His many masterpieces, including *David, Day and Night, Madonna of Bruges, Twilight and Dawn, La Pieta, Medici Madonna and Child,* and his towering statue of *Moses,* have inspired mankind for four hundred years.

And yet Michelangelo was never satisfied with his work! After completing his *Moses,* acclaimed as his greatest work, the master sculptor surveyed his work and then suddenly in anger he struck the knee of his statue with his chisel, crying, "Why dost thou not speak?" Here was a man whose ideal was to make cold marble come to life!

Today we can see the long, narrow dent on the knee of Michelangelo's *Moses.* It is the trademark of a man who never realized the perfection of his dream. It is the mark of a man who had set his ideal among the stars. It is a symbol of the fact that men becomes masters by attempting the impossible, and by never permitting themselves to be lulled to sleep by the ether of self-satisfaction.

Only little men are ever satisfied with their acomplishments—that's why they remain little. The big men are never satisfied—that's why they become great.

The Friendly Adventurer in Sunshine Magazine

ELBERT HUBBARD LOOKS AT LIFE

Charity: a thing that begins at home, and usually stays there.

Editor: a person employed on a newspaper, whose business it is to separate the wheat from the chaff, and to see that the chaff is printed.

Friend: one who knows all about you and loves you just the same.

No man needs a vacation so much as the person who has just had one.

The object of teaching a child is to enable him to get along without a teacher.

Righteous indignation: your own wrath as opposed to the shocking bad temper of others.

THE DESPAIR OF LONELINESS

One evening in 1808, a gaunt, sad-faced man entered the offices of Dr. James Hamilton in Manchester, England. The doctor was struck by the melancholy appearance of his visitor. He inquired:

"Are you sick?"

"Yes, doctor, sick of a mortal malady."

"What malady?"

"I am frightened of the terror of the world around me. I am depressed by life. I can find no happiness anywhere, nothing amuses me, and I have nothing to live for. If you can't help me, I shall kill myself."

"The malady is not mortal. You only need to get out of yourself. You need to laugh; to get some pleasure from life."

"What shall I do?"

"Go to the circus tonight to see Grimaldi, the clown. Grimaldi is the funniest man alive. He'll cure you."

A spasm of pain crossed the poor man's face as he said: "Doctor, don't jest with me; I am Grimaldi."

John Summerfield Wimbish

I DO THE BEST I KNOW HOW

Abraham Lincoln once said, "If I tried to read, much less answer, all the criticisms made of me, and all the attacks leveled against me, this office would have to be closed for all other business. I do the best I know how, the very best I can. And I mean to keep on doing this, down to the very end. If the end brings me out all wrong, ten angels swearing I had been right would make no difference. If the end brings me out all right, then what is said against me now will not amount to anything."

SAMUEL JOHNSON'S VIEWS

Adversity is the state in which a man most easily becomes acquainted with himself, being especially free from admirers then.

He was dull in a new way, and that made many think him great.

I hate mankind, for I think myself one of the best of them, and I know how bad I am.

If he does really think that there is no distinction between vice and virtue, when he leaves our house let us count our spoons.

Nothing flatters a man as much as the happiness of his wife; he is always proud of himself as the source of it.

Patron: commonly a wretch who supports with insolence, and is paid with flattery.

Treating your adversary with respect is giving him an advantage to which he is not entitled.

STRANGE

Famous violinist Jascha Heifetz tells an amusing story of an occasion when, at a party one night, his host introduced him to a professional boxer.

Remarked the violinist: "I see we are both in the same business. Both of us earn our living with our hands."

The boxer looked at the violinist's hands and face with admiration.

"Gosh," he exclaimed, "you must be pretty good. There's not a mark on you!"   *Tit-Bits, London*

ONE MORE ROUND

Of the many statements made by the late James J. Corbett during his colorful career, one is pre-eminent. "What," someone asked him, "is most important for a man to do to become champion?" And Corbett replied: "Fight one more round."

Corbett was a champion of the prize ring, but there have been champions in other fields, and the same has held true of them. They have been able to fight "one more round."

Thomas Edison, seeking a proper filament to light his incandescent lamp, failed month after month—but one day his efforts met success, and the world was presented with the electric light. He had fought "one more round."

S. N. Behrman, an American playwright, turned out manuscripts for 11 years before he finally sold his first play. Somerset Maugham was a failure for ten years, earning $500 in all that time. A producer, needing a play to fill in while he was looking around, dug Maugham's forgotten "Lady Frederick" out of a desk drawer. Maugham became the toast of London.

Enrico Caruso was told by his music teacher that he had no voice. He persevered for a dozen years, studying at night while he worked in a factory during the day. His opportunity came—but his voice cracked during rehearsal, and he fled from the theater in tears. When he filled in one night for a tenor who had become ill, the audience hissed him. But he continued to study. He reached the top.

When Walt Disney applied at the *Kansas City Star* for a job as an artist, the editor told him he didn't have any talent, and sent him away, urging him to give it up. Even his first series of animated cartoons, "Oswald the Rabbit" failed. Then came Mickey Mouse.

Zane Grey didn't sell a story during his first five years as a writer. H. G. Wells was discharged from his first job—after a month as a dry-goods salesman.

The first time George Gershwin played the piano in public, the audience laughed him off the stage. Even as a composer, he met with disheartening discouragement, writing almost a hundred melodies before he sold his first—for $5.

Penniless Carrie Jacobs Bond, semi-invalid, tried hand-painted china—even singing songs in vaudeville. Bitter failure was her lot. She tried song writing—and publishers would not buy. Then, like James J. Corbett, she fought "one more round." She wrote "The End of a Perfect Day."
Adapted from Louis Sobol in New York Journal and American

EPIGRAMS OF OSCAR LEVANT

I've given up reading books; I find it takes my mind off myself.

The first thing I do in the morning is brush my teeth and sharpen my tongue.

A pun is the lowest form of humor—when you don't think of it first.

A LITTLE AT A TIME

John Erskine, well-known author, professor, and lecturer, once wrote that he learned the most valuable lesson of his life when he was fourteen. His piano teacher asked him how much he practiced, and how long at a stretch. The boy replied that he practiced for an hour or more at a time.

"Don't do that," warned the teacher. "When you grow up, time won't come in long stretches. Practice in minutes, whenever you can find them—five or ten before school, after lunch, between chores. Spread the practice throughout the day, and music will become a part of your life."

The observance of this advice enabled Erskine to live a comparatively complete life as a creative writer, outside his regular duties as an instructor. He wrote most of his *Helen of Troy,* his most famous work, while commuting between his home and the university.   *Sunshine Magazine*

POINT OF VIEW

A reporter, interviewing Lionel Barrymore, asked him if he still found acting as much fun as it used to be.

The great actor snorted, "Look, son, I'm 75 years old. Nothing is as much fun as it used to be."

United Mine Workers Journal

THE TRAINING OF PRESIDENTS

Andrew Johnson was the only President of the United States who had no formal schooling whatsoever. It is said that his wife taught him to read and write. Two-thirds of the Presidents have been college graduates.   *Sunshine Magazine*

WIT AND WISDOM OF GEORGE BERNARD SHAW

The British churchgoer prefers a severe preacher because he thinks a few home truths will do his neighbours no harm.

England and America are two countries separated by the same language.

Few people think more than two or three times a year; I have made an international reputation for myself by thinking once or twice a week.

I enjoy convalescence; it is the part that makes the illness worth while.

The liar's punishment is not in the least that he is not believed, but that he cannot believe anyone else.

There may be some doubt as to who are the best people to have charge of children, but there can be no doubt that parents are the worst.

EVERYTHING THAT LIVES

Several years ago a widely distributed advertisement of the John Hancock Mutual Life Insurance Company presented this stirring interpretation of American independence:

There was once a man who loved Nature with such a deep and moving love that she told him one of her secrets. She gave him the power to create new plants.

The man, whose name was Luther Burbank, would go into his garden and walk softly among the growing things therein.

He saw that every plant was a child. It had its own face, its own promise, its unique touch of genius or character. And if that promise were tended and encouraged, the plant would grow more useful and beautiful each year. Luther Burbank puttered in his garden for fifty years for the greater happiness of all people.

He made potatoes grow larger, whiter, more delicious than they had ever been. He taught the cactus of the desert to throw away its spines, so that cattle could fatten upon it, and made the blackberry shed its thorns, so it would not cut the fingers of the pickers.

For him, the plum grew without pits, and strawberries ripened all year. Trees learned to shelter their fruit from frost, and walnuts wore thinner shells which the small hands of children could open.

The daisy grew more beautiful for him, and the amaryllis burst into flame; the calla lily wore perfume, and the dahlia found new fragrance. He left the earth covered with flowers and fruits that no one had ever attempted to grow before. And all because he knew a secret.

He knew that everything that lives has the power to become greater—if it is free to put forth the best that is in it. This is a truth long known in America, where every man's promise can reach its finest flower, growing in the kindly soil of freedom.

Sunshine Magazine

OF COURSE NOT

Former President Coty, of France, is in great demand as an after-dinner speaker because of his sharp wit.

At a banquet a lovely English-woman who was his neighbor said: "Tell me, Mr. President, are Parisiennes really more charming than any other women?"

Said Coty without hesitation: "They are, indeed, madam. Why? Because a Parisienne has the beauty of a rosebud when she's twenty, the bewitching quality of a love song when she's thirty, and is quite perfect at forty."

"And after forty?" the English-woman asked.

"Madam," replied the President, "a true Parisienne is never more than forty, whatever her age!"   *Tit-Bits, London*

PERSISTENCE

Mark Twain often told about an elderly Mississippi pilot who had retired from active work on the river, and had finally reached his one hundredth birthday. Mark Twain called on him as the representative of a St. Louis newspaper, and asked the centenarian how he accounted for his longevity.

The old man replied with the usual remarks about avoiding bad habits and cultivating good ones.

Mark protested that he had known a man who followed exactly the same regimen, yet lived only to eighty years. "How do you account for that?" he asked the pilot.

The wise old man answered calmly, "He didn't keep it up long enough."

COMMENTS OF THE WITTY SIDNEY SMITH

He has occasional flashes of silence that make his conversation perfectly delightful.

He has returned from Italy a greater bore than ever; he bores on architecture, painting, statuary, and music.

He has spent all his life in letting down buckets into empty wells; and he is frittering away his age in trying to draw them up again.

I am convinced digestion is the great secret of life.

You and I are exceptions to the laws of nature; you have risen by your gravity, and I have sunk by my levity.

HIS FIRST WORRY

One of Henry Ward Beecher's favorite stories was about a young man who was applying for a job in a New England factory. Asking for the owner, he found himself in the presence of a nervous, fidgety man who looked hopelessly dyspeptic. "The only vacancy here," he told the applicant, "is a vice-presidency. The man that takes the job must shoulder all my cares."

"That's a tough job," said the applicant. "What's the salary?"

"I'll pay you ten thousand a year if you will really take over all my worries."

"Where is the ten thousand coming from?" asked the applicant, suspiciously.

"That, my friend," replied the owner, "is your first worry."

THE FORCE OF PRAYER

The spectacle of a nation praying is more awe-inspiring than the explosion of an atomic bomb. The force of prayer is greater than any possible combination of man-made or man-controlled powers, because prayer is man's greatest means of trapping the infinite resources of God.

J. Edgar Hoover, Director Federal Bureau
of Investigation, Department of Justice

NO PURPOSE

Once, when General Ulysses S. Grant was visiting Scotland, his host gave him a demonstration of a game, new to Grant, called golf. Carefully, the host placed the ball on the tee and took a mighty swing, sending chunks of turf flying but not touching the ball.

Grant watched the exhibition quietly, but after the sixth unsuccessful attempt to hit the ball, he turned to his perspiring, embarrassed host and commented: "There seems to be a fair amount of exercise in the game, but I fail to see the purpose of the ball."

WITTICISMS OF OSCAR WILDE

All women become like their mothers—that is their tragedy; no man does—that's his.

Anybody can make history; only a great man can write it.

Anyone can sympathize with the sufferings of a friend, but it requires a very fine nature to sympathize with a friend's success.

Arguments are extremely vulgar, for everybody in good society holds exactly the same opinions.

Bernard Shaw is an excellent man; he has not an enemy in the world, and none of his friends like him.

The difference between literature and journalism is that journalism is unreadable and literature is unread.

Duty is what one expects from others.

Fashion is a form of ugliness so intolerable that we have to alter it every six months.

A gentleman is one who never hurts anyone's feelings unintentionally.

George Moore wrote brilliant English until he discovered grammar.

He was always late on principle, his principle being that punctuality is the thief of time.

I like Wagner's music better than anybody's; it is so loud, one can talk the whole time without other people hearing what one says.

I never put off till tomorrow what I can possibly do the day after.

In America, the young are always ready to give to those who are older than themselves the full benefits of their inexperience.

Insincerity is merely a method by which we can multiply our personalities.

It is perfectly monstrous the way people go about nowadays saying things against one, behind one's back, that are absolutely and entirely true.

Land gives one position, and prevents one from keeping it up.

The longer I live the more keenly I feel that whatever was good enough for our fathers is not good enough for us.

My own business always bores me to death; I prefer other people's.

The public is wonderfully tolerant—it forgives everything except genius.

To love oneself is the beginning of a lifelong romance.

When I was young I used to think that money was the most important thing in life; now that I am old, I know it is.

TWO FORCES WHICH MOVE US

America is fortunate to have the genius and loyalties of Dr. Wernher von Braun, world-famed scientist, as head of the Army's top civilian rocket agency.

In his early teens, when reading about the stars and outer space, he embraced the idea that rocket power might one day carry man beyond the earth's atmosphere. He fired his first rudimentary rockets from the city dump near Berlin when he was 18. . . .

In large measure the first U.S. Earth satellite was the direct result of his wizardy and that of the 120 German scientists and technicians who migrated with him to the Army's Ballistic Missile Agency where he is Director of Development Operations. He is still motivated by his boyhood dreams of space conquest and believes that, with a coordinated program, space travel can be achieved within ten years.

Dr. von Braun is a practical man who works in cold facts and figures and it is this man who made this extraordinary statement to the New York Herald Tribune:

"Survival—yours and mine and our children's—depends on our adherence to ethical principles. Ethics alone will decide whether atomic energy will be an earthly blessing or the source of mankind's utter destruction.

"Where does the desire for ethical action come from? What makes us want to be ethical? I believe there are two forces which move us.

—One is belief in a Last Judgment, when every one of us has to account for what we did with God's great gift of life on earth.

—The other is belief in an immortal soul, a soul which will cherish the award or suffer the penalty decreed in a final judgment.

"Belief in God and in immortality thus gives us the moral strength and the ethical guidance we need for virtually every action in our daily lives.

"In our modern world people seem to feel that science has somehow made such 'religious ideas' seem untimely or old-fashioned.

"But I think science has a real surprise for the skeptics. Science, for instance, tells us that nothing in nature, not even the tiniest particle, can disappear without a trace.

"Think about that for a moment. Once you do, your thoughts about life will never be the same.

"Science has found that nothing can disappear without a trace. Nature does not know extinction. All it knows is transformation!

"Now, if God applies this fundamental principle to the most

minute and insignificant parts of His universe doesn't it make sense to assume that He applies it also to the masterpiece of His creation—the human soul? I think it does. And everything science has taught me—and continues to teach me—strengthens my belief in the continuity of our spiritual existence after death. Nothing disappears without a trace."

Dr. von Braun's many hours spent bending to the telescope and searching the heavens have given him insight and knowledge passing that of most mortals.

Phyllis H. Moehrle, The Calvary Pulpit

CHAPTER IV

HUMOROUS STORIES

PRECOCIOUS CHILD

The gentleman stopped to talk to the wee girl who was making mud pies on the sidewalk.

"My word," he exclaimed, "you're pretty dirty, aren't you, my little girl?"

"Yes," she replied, "but I'm prettier clean."

ACCOMMODATING

The patient complained bitterly, "Five dollars is a lot of money for pulling a tooth—just two seconds' work."

"Well," replied the dentist consolingly, "if you wish, I can pull it very slowly."

HE SHOULD KNOW

The burglars were busy in the clothing store.

"Look at the price of this suit!" exclaimed one. "Downright robbery, if you ask me!"

LET'S BE REASONABLE

"I resent your remark," said the fifth grader, "an' I'll give you just five seconds to take it back!"

"Oh, yeah!" snarled the seventh grader. "Suppose I don't take it back in five seconds?"

"Well," said the first, more meekly, "how much time do you want?"

SMART CHIEF

A visitor to a western hotel asked the clerk about the weather. The clerk had no information, but an Indian standing nearby came up with the answer, "Going rain—much." And it did.

Awed by the Indian's weather-accuracy, the visitor sought him out the next day for another prediction, and learned it was to be clear and cool. Again the forecast was correct.

The third morning the query was repeated, but this time the Indian smiled and said, "Dunno—radio busted."

WHAT'S WRONG

Roared the politician to the editor: "What do you mean by publicly insulting me in your old rag of a paper? I will not stand for it, and I demand an immediate apology!"

"Just a moment," answered the editor. "Didn't the news item appear exactly as you gave it to us—that you had resigned as city treasurer?"

"It did, but where did you put it?—in the column under the heading, 'Public Improvements'!"

STRANGE

Little Eldon, fretting at the teacher's assignment, asked skeptically, "Do you get paid for teaching us?"

The teacher smiled. "Yes."

Puzzled, the boy exclaimed, "That's funny! We do all the work!"

BUSY

A traveling salesman dropped in on a bank officer whose desk was covered with letters, papers, magazines, and miscellany.

The banker was busily engaged in writing a memo, and greeted the salesman with: "I'm very busy this morning, very busy!"

Glancing at the desk, the salesman replied: "Well, I'm glad to know that; I thought you were just confused."

THE BILL

The stork is a bird with a great big bill. He brings us the babies whenever he will. Then comes the doctor, and when he is through, you find that he has a big bill, too!

IT WORKS

Mrs. Smith: "I always feel lots better after a good cry."

Mrs. Jones: "So do I. It sort of gets things out of my system."

Mrs. Smith: "No, it doesn't get anything out of my system, but it does get things out of my husband."

HE EARNED IT

Small boy: "Could I please have two balloons?"

Advertiser: "Well, usually we give just one balloon to each youngster. Do you have a brother at home?"

Small boy: "No, but my sister has. I want it for him."

THAT WILL LEARN YOU

Roses are red; I'm black and blue. If you went skating, you would be, too!

THE WAY WARS START

This younger generation of ours is plenty smart. Take the boy who asked his father how wars got started.

"Well," said Dad, "suppose America persisted in quarreling with England, and—"

"But," interrupted the mother, "America must never quarrel with England."

"I know," said the father, "but I am only taking a hypothetical instance."

"But you are misleading the child," protested the mother.

"No, I am not," shouted the father angrily.

"Never mind, Dad," put in the boy; "I think I know how wars start."

BE CAREFUL HOW YOU ANSWER

Nina (to her wailing son): "Mommy's sorry she ran over your bicycle, dear, but what on earth was it doing in the flower garden?"

BUILT TO ORDER

"This looks very complicated for a child," the mother said to the salesman in the toy store.

"It's an educational toy, designed to adjust a child to live in the world today," the clerk explained. "Any way he puts it together, it's wrong."

HALF SUCCESSFUL

A clergyman once preached a sermon to his flock which was designed to persuade them that it is the duty of the rich to help the poor.

He was telling a friend about it, and the latter asked: "Did you convince them?"

"The sermon was 50 per cent successful," replied the minister. "I convinced the poor."

POINT OF VIEW

Ivan Demetrius and Mischa Petrovitz loved to argue. Standing on a street corner in Moscow, they watched an infantry regiment marching by.

"Do men grow upward or downward?" asked Ivan absently.

"Why, downward, of course," replied Mischa.

"How do you know, Mischa?" asked Ivan.

"Because," replied Mischa, "once when I outgrew my overcoat, it became too short for me at the bottom."

"No, Mischa," replied Ivan, looking out at the marching soldiers, "men grow upward."

"Why do you say that, Ivan?"

"Because," replied Ivan, "you will see that our brothers marching out there are all even at the bottom, but uneven at the top."

PRETTY BAD JOKE

Mo: "Did you know that all radio announcers have small hands?"

Jo: "How's that?"

Mo: "Wee paws for station identification.

WHAT'S IT ALL ABOUT?

Rushin' to the office, rushin' out to eat, rushin' back and rushin' home down the rushin' street.

Rushin' up and rushin' down, rushin' in and out. Say, what's all this rushin' for? What's it all about?

HE WORKS, TOO

A newcomer to Washington telephoned the Labor Department and was greeted by the switchboard operator's traditional "This is Labor."

The newsman snorted softly. "Well, honey," he replied, "I ain't resting either."

A SLIGHT DIFFERENCE

"When I was once in danger from a lion," said the big-game hunter, "I tried sitting down and staring at him, as I had lost my gun. The lion didn't even touch me."

"Strange! How do you explain that?"

"Well," mused the hunter, "it must have been because I was sitting on a high branch of a tall tree."   *Tit-Bits, London*

AN IDEA FOR DECORATORS

Once there was a woman who wanted her apartment done over while she was out of town. This woman was very fussy and insisted everything be the exact shade she specified. To help the painters, she left an ash tray as a sample of the special shade she wanted the ceiling painted.

After trying to mix the exact shade she specified, the painters finally hit upon the solution—they painted the ash tray, then the ceiling. When the woman returned, she was delighted with the perfect match the painters had obtained.

IS THAT CLEAR?

Office Manager (on the telephone): "The name is Zander. Zander! Zander! Z! Z! No, not C. A-B-C-D-E-F-G-H-I-J-K-L-M-N-O-P-Q-R-S-T-U-V-W-X-Y—Z! Z!"

OPTIMIST—PESSIMIST

"I had a surprise this morning," said the optimist. "I put on a last summer's suit and in one of the pockets I found a big roll of bills which I had entirely forgotten."

"I'll bet none of them were receipted," said the pessimist.

WRONG VERSION

A London teacher recently reported the excuse of a little girl who said she could not prepare her Bible reading for the school assembly "because the only copy we have at home is the reversed version."

LET'S FORGET THE WHOLE THING

A farmer was the week-end guest of a man who owned extensive parkland, stables, and prize cattle. On his first morning at the house the maid who brought him his hot water asked about breakfast. "Tea, coffee, or milk?" she asked.

"Tea," he answered.

"Very good, sir," she replied, "and will you take Ceylon, China, or Assam?"

He didn't know anything about Assam, so he chose that.

"With milk, cream or lemon?"

"Milk," he said and thought the matter was settled.

"Yes, sir," said the maid. "Jersey, Guernsey, or Alderney?"

HER EXCUSE

A little girl in the 2nd grade had been told to bring her birth certificate at the opening of school. She was found by the teacher, sobbing in her seat. When asked what the trouble was, she said: "I forgot to bring my excuse for being born."

John C. Middlekauff, Pulpit Digest

AN IDEA

Benjamin Fairless was once advised by the Federation of Women Stockholders to go on a diet. They suggested he might begin by hiring a "sit-in" to take his place at 6-course banquets. "All leaders have to take it on the chin," said President Wilma Soss, "but one chin is enough."

HE TOLD THE TRUTH

Three sailors were spending their leave in the country. Presently two of them got into a heated argument over what kind of an animal a heifer was.

"It's a sort of pig," said one.

"Not on your life," replied the other; "it's a kind of sheep."

Finally they called in the third sailor.

"Bill," said the first sailor, "Wot's a heifer—is it a pig or a sheep?"

Bill pondered over the matter. "To tell you the truth, mates," he said, "I dunno much about poultry."

OF COURSE

A small boy was inviting his friend to his birthday party, and explained how to find the apartment in which he lived. "Come to the seventh floor," he said, "and where you see the letter D on the door, push the button with your elbow and when the door opens put your foot against it."

"Why do I have to use my elbow and my foot?" asked the invited guest.

"Well, I suppose you'd have your hands full of somethin', since it's my birthday."

CREDIT

The following sign is said to be prominently displayed in a coffee shop in Milwaukee:

"You want credit—I no give, you get sore. You want credit—I give, you no pay, I get sore. Better you get sore."

POETRY?

Beneath the spreading chestnut tree the village smithie snoozes; no nag, since 1923, has been to him for shoeses.

CONCEIT

Once a feature writer, so top-flight that his newspaper let him fall into the habit of writing the pronoun "I" as often as he liked, re-read proudly his by-lined Easter feature in the Sunday issue. Monday morning, on the newsroom bulletin board an anonymous copyreader posted the score:

Jesus—13
"I"—21.   *Prof. Roscoe Ellard, in Editor & Publisher*

AGREED

Speaker: "The time has come, fellow citizens, when we must get rid of socialism, and communism, and anarchism—"

Aged listener: "Let's throw out rheumatism, too!"

NO PARKING

In a Kansas town, motorists who ignored "No Parking" signs in front of a church refrained from parking there when the signs were changed to read, "Thou Shalt Not Park!" They probably thought a new commandment was added to the original ten.

MODERN AGE

The newest dream kitchen has a lounge with TV, bookcase and fireplace, but most women would chuck the whole thing for a good, old-fashioned hired girl.   *Changing Times*

ANALYZE HIS ANATOMY

A pupil in the poetry class was asked to write a short verse using the words "analyze" and "anatomy." Here is what he wrote:

> "My analyze over the ocean,
> My analyze over the sea,
> My analyze over the ocean—
> O, bring back my ana-to-my!"

SIMPLE

All summer Paul watched Eddie give demonstrations on how to putt. Ed, who sometimes wears glasses, seldom missed a putt, even from the edge of the green. Finally, at the end of the summer, Paul asked how he holed out so accurately. "Well," said Ed, "these glasses of mine are bifocals. When I line up a putt, I look through the edges of the two lenses so I see two balls, one small and one big. Then it's simple. I just knock the small ball in the big hole."

THAT SETTLES IT

Theatre Arts records this conversation between a man who dialed "Information" for their number, and the operator.

"I'm sorry, sir, but there is no one listed by the name of Theodore Arts."

"It's not a person; it's a magazine—*Theatre Arts.*"

"There is no listing for Theodore Arts."

"Not *Theodore* Arts—*Theatre* Arts. T-h-e-a-t-r-e."

"That," said the operator with scornful finality, "is not the way to spell Theodore."

DECISIVE

Psychiatrist: "Do you have trouble making up your mind?"
Patient: "Well—yes and no."

A PLACE FOR EVERYTHING

Joe: "I certainly am strong for these labor-saving devices. I don't have any trouble finding my collar buttons now. I always find them in one certain place."

Bill: "Where is that?"

Joe: "In the vacuum cleaner."

IT'S HARD TO PRONOUNCE

Some Americans were dining in a French restaurant, and one of them wanted some horse-radish, but didn't know how to ask for it. "I know the French for 'horse' is 'cheval,'" he said, "and 'red' I suppose is 'rouge.' Now if I only knew the French for 'ish,' I could ask for some."

LONG WAY?

An Easterner was being driven by a rancher over a blistering and almost barren stretch of West Texas when a large brightly colored bird scurried across the road in front of them. The visitor asked what it was.

"That's a bird of paradise," said the rancher.

"Pretty long way from home, isn't he?" remarked the visitor.

HEAD OF THE CLASS

The teacher wrote the following sentence on the blackboard and asked her pupils to paraphrase it:

"He was bent on seeing her."

Little Willie turned in this paraphrase:

"The sight of her doubled him up."

A DIPLOMAT

At a reception in Washington a young man was asked by a widow to guess her age. "You must have some idea," she said, as he hesitated.

"I have several ideas," he admitted, with a smile. "The trouble is that I hesitate whether to make it ten years younger on account of your looks, or ten years older on account of your intelligence." *Capper's Farmer*

LUCKY

The two sat in the moonlight, contemplating the future. Half jovial, half serious, she exclaimed: "The man I marry must be brave as a lion, but not forward; handsome as Apollo, but not conceited; wise as Solomon, but meek as a lamb; a man who is kind to every woman, but loves only me."

Whereupon he exclaimed: "How lucky we met!"

ABOUT TIME

My little friend Billie was about 4 years old and had a little dog. They were playing in my yard and I offered Billie 3 cents for his dog. He said, "No." However, after building me up, cent by cent, to 7 cents, he sold it to me. I then told him that he knew I was 80 years old, lived alone, and of course could not keep the dog at my place. I told him to keep it, and in fact should go right on calling the dog his. Some six months later I was painting the front steps, and over come Billie. I gave him a little brush and he painted away on the lower step. After a while he looked up and said:

"Don't you think it is about time for you to buy some of the dog food for your dog?"

IT WORKS

A man who was always happy, was asked how he kept in such a jovial mood, although he had so many troubles. His answer was, "I long ago learned to cooperate with the inevitable."

GOOD IDEA

The colored maid met the caller at the door. "Miss Alice, she ain't home," was the reply to the caller's inquiry. "She's gone down to de class."

"What class?" asked the caller.

"Miss Alice she's fixin' to git married, you know, an' she's takin' lessons in domestic silence."

THE WHOLE STORY

A schoolboy was asked to write an essay on cats, and here is what he wrote:

"Cats that's meant for little boys to maul and tease is called Maultese cats. Some cats is rekernized by how quiet their purs is, and these is named Persian cats. The cats what has very bad tempers is called Angorie cats. And cats with deep feelin's is called Feline cats. I don't like cats."

NOT OVERWEIGHT

A woman stepped off the penny scales and turned to her husband.

"What is the verdict? A little overweight?" he asked.

"No, no," she replied, "but according to that height table, I should be about six inches taller."

IT COULD BE

A fly's a fly because he flies; a flea's a flea beause he fleas; a bee's a bee because he bees!

PAST EXPERIENCE

A woman posed for a picture in front of the fallen pillars of an ancient temple in Greece.

"Don't get the car into the picture," she instructed the photographer, "or my husband will think I ran into the place."

EFFICIENCY EXPERTS

Former President Hoover once gave his opinion of "efficiency experts." One arrived in a snowstorm to take over a job in the mid-west. He was met at the station by an Irishman who seated the expert in a sleigh and wrapped a buffalo robe about him. "Don't you know," objected the visitor, "that the cold is kept out more efficiently if the leather is on the outside?" The Irishman meditated, "I wonder why nobody ever told that to the buffaloes!"

SMART YOUNGSTER

A mother took her 7-year-old daughter to a very progressive school. Among the questions asked was this: "Are you a little girl or a little boy?"

The little girl replied, "I'm a boy."

The teacher went on at a great rate, scaring the mother to

death by saying the child was psychologically confused, should be put with a group of problem children, and so forth. On the way home the mother said, "Darling, why did you say you were a little boy?"

Her daughter gave her a long look. "When anybody asks me a dumb question," she said, "they deserve a dumb answer."

THEY GENERALLY SUCCEED

The hardest task of a girl's life is to prove to a man that his intentions really are serious.

THE PAUSE THAT REFRESHES

A famous ballet dancer constantly confounded his public with his amazing leaps, which were marvels of beauty.

"How do you do them?" asked a friend one night, after watching from the wings.

"Oh, it's quite simple," replied the dancer. "All you have to do is jump into the air—and pause a little."

HEAR! HEAR!

The customer settled himself and let the barber put the towel around him. Then he told the barber, "Before we start, I know the weather's awful. I don't care who wins the next big fight, and I don't bet on the horse races. I know I'm getting thin on top, but I don't mind. Now get on with it!"

"Well, sir, if you don't mind," said the barber, "I'll be able to concentrate better if you don't talk so much."   *Link*

ADVICE TO TOURISTS

A tourist in Switzerland was taken by a local guide on a mountain climb. At one point the guide disturbed his client by urging: "Be careful not to fall here because it is very dangerous. But if you do fall, remember to look to the right—the view is the best for miles around."   *Tit-Bits, London*

DIPLOMAT

"Two!" shouted the pint-sized umpire.

"Two what?" snarled the big catcher.

"Yeah, 2 what?" echoed the equally large batter.

"Too close to tell," said the umpire.

CORRECT

A physics professor called on one of his students to list some characteristics of heat and cold.

"Things expand in heat and contract in cold," answered the student.

"Give an example."

"In summer," answered the student, "the days are long and in winter the days are short."

SHE UNDERSTOOD

A young bride decided to try a chicken dinner for her husband. She talked lengthily with the butcher, who finally backed up his guarantee of the chicken's quality with a money-back offer and a flowery exposition of its fine points.

"I'll take one then—about 4 pounds," the bride agreed.

"Shall I draw it for you?" asked the butcher.

"No, thank you," she answered brightly, "your description of it will be quite sufficient."

THEY ALWAYS DO

Mrs. Busybody was pumping the local doctor about the demise of the town's richest man. "You knew him well," she cooed. "How much wealth did he leave?"

With a tip of his hat, the old doctor replied, "All of it, madam, all of it."   *Capper's Weekly*

IT CERTAINLY DOES

Rubbing elbows with a man will reveal things about him you never before realized. The same thing is true of rubbing fenders.   *Arcadia (Wis.) News-Leader*

HOW'S THAT

"Hello, Sam," exclaimed Jim, meeting a buddy for the first time since the war's end. "Did you marry that girl you used to go with, or are you still doing your own cooking and ironing?"

"Yes," replied Sam.

NO GOOD WAY OUT

Modern psychology tells us that it's bad to be an orphan, terrible to be an only child, damaging to be the youngest, crushing to be in the middle, and taxing to be the oldest. There seems no way out, except to be born an adult.

HE KNEW

Mother and daughter were in the kitchen washing dishes, while Father and 7-year-old Warren were in the living room reading the evening paper. Suddenly there sounded a crash of falling dishes. Father and Warren listened expectantly in the ensuing silence. "It was Mother," Warren finally announced.

"How do you know?" Father inquired.

"Because," answered Warren firmly, "she isn't saying anything."

THEY NEVER DO

It looked as tho both the hero and the heroine of the Western movie were doomed. They were surrounded completely by angry redmen. One of the little boys in the front row sniffed, "If he had kept his eye on the Indians instead of the girl, this never would have happened."

CAUTION AND COWARDICE

"What is the difference," asked the teacher, "between caution and cowardice?"

Johnny, who observed things carefully for so youthful a person, answered: "Caution is when you're afraid, and cowardice is when the other fellow's afraid."

ABSENT MINDED

There was something the absent-minded professor badly wanted to do that night and he sat up late beating his brains to remember what it was. Around two o'clock in the morning it suddenly came to him: He wanted to go to bed early!

THE MOSTEST

Waiter: "I assure you, sir, this is the best restaurant in town. If you order eggs, you get the freshest; if you order hot soup, you get the hottest."

Customer: "I believe you're right. I ordered a small steak."

SMART SALESMAN

A boy who usually earned extra money mowing lawns was slow about leaving his house one Saturday morning, and his father asked him why. "Oh," he answered, "I'm waiting till they get started. I get most of my work from people who are already half way thru."

A SAD TALE

Three polar bears were sitting on an iceberg. All were cold and quiet. Finally the father bear said, "Now I've a tale to tell."

"I, too, have a tale to tell," said the mother bear.

The little polar bear looked up at his parents, and said, "My tale is told!"

BE CAREFUL

A story is told of Hugh Cullen, of Houston, a generous bene-factor of the University of Houston. When he announced a $5 million gift to the University, the *Houston Chronicle* is sup-posed to have reported he gave $15 million. Cullen called Jesse Jones, publisher of the *Chronicle,* so the story goes, and said, "O.K., Jesse, I'll make it fifteen, since you said so—but don't let it happen again!"   *Barron's*

LOST

In the shopping crowd a young lady was accosted by a small girl who had lost her mother. " 'Scuse me, please," she asked, "but have you seen a lady in a green coat without a little girl that looks like me?"

TO THE HEAD OF THE CLASS

"Touchdown" Sanders, football player for a southern school, was having trouble with his grades. Since he was the star player on the team his services were needed. He was called into the president's office for re-examination. The school decided to give the boy a one-question examination, and since he was from Florida, the question was: "What is the capital of Florida?"

"Touchdown" sweated over this for some time, and finally wrote "Monticello." Yes, he passed. In checking the answer, the officials said that 100 was perfect, and Monticello is 25 miles from Tallahassee. Twenty-five from 100 leaves 75—and 75 is passing! *Capper's Weekly*

ALMOST MADE IT

Thomas Edison hated formal dinners, which always seemed stuffy affairs to him. One night at a particularly dull gathering, he decided to sneak away to his laboratory.

As he was pacing back and forth near the door, waiting for an opportunity to escape, his host came up.

"It certainly is a delight to see you, Mr. Edison," he said. "What are you working on now?"

"My exit," replied the inventor.

HIS MISTAKE

Prisoner to fellow inmate: "I was making big money—about a quarter of an inch too big."

PROFOUND

When both a speaker and an audience are confused the speech is profound. *Banking*

THE MULE

"The mule," wrote a schoolboy, "is a hardier bird than a goose or turkey, and different. He wears his wings on the side of his head. He has two legs to walk with, two more to kick with, and is usually awful backward about going forward."

HIS EXCUSE

Two men fishing on a Sunday morning were feeling pretty guilty, especially since the fish didn't bite. One said to the other, "I guess I should have stayed home, and gone to church."

To which the other angler replied lazily, "I couldn't have gone to church anyway; my wife's sick in bed."

The Keystone Butler

WHAT HE EXPECTED

Said Mother: "Aunt Becky won't kiss you with that dirty face." Said Small Boy: "That's what I figured."

DON'T WE ALL?

Teacher: "How do you spell 'inconsequentially'?"
Willie: "Wrong."

HE KNEW

The teacher was checking her students' knowledge of proverbs.

"Cleanliness is next to what?" she asked.

A small boy replied with real feeling: "Impossible!"

CORRECT

A farmer had a wife who was very critical of his grammar. One evening he told her he had a friend named Bill he would like for her to meet.

"Don't call him Bill," she insisted. "Call him William."

When the friend arrived, the farmer said, "Let me tell you a tale."

"Not tale," the wife interrupted. "Say anecdote."

That night, upon retiring, the farmer told her to put out the light.

"Not put out," she exclaimed, "say extinguish the light."

Later in the night she awakened her husband and sent him downstairs to investigate a noise.

When he returned, she asked him what it was.

"It was," he explained carefully, "a William-goat which I took by its anecdote and extinguished."

NOW HE WILL PAY

A lawyer sent an overdue bill to a client, attaching a note which said, "This bill is one year old."

By return mail the lawyer had his bill back. To it was attached another note: "Happy birthday."

TAXES

Salesman to customer examining a television set: "The tag refers to city, state and federal taxes, madam. The price is additional."

COME ANYWAY

When a flood washed out the railroad to a small city where he was scheduled to make an address, the late vice-president Charles G. Dawes telegraphed the chairman of the committee: "Cannot arrive on time. Washout on line."

He was nonplussed to receive the forthcoming answer: "Never mind wash. Buy another shirt at our expense and come anyway."

THE REASON?

Two cronies, one 50 and one 60 years of age, were arguing about the forthcoming marriage of the latter to a young lady in her 20's.

"I don't believe in these May and December marriages," said the younger. "After all, December is going to find in May the freshness and beauty of springtime, but whatever is May going to find in December?"

The bridegroom-to-be chuckled at this and replied with a sly wink, "Christmas."

GOOD EXCUSE

"You haven't returned your report card yet, Johnny," admonished teacher, "and it's three weeks overdue."

"I know," admitted the pupil, "but I can't get it back."

"What do you mean, 'can't get it back'?" demanded the teacher.

"Well, you see, you gave me two A's and Mother and Dad are still passing it around to the relatives."

THANKS

"Have I told you about my grandchildren?"
"No, and I appreciate it."

AND HURRY UP

Her husband being slightly indisposed, a young and inexperienced wife attempted to take his temperature. In a state of great excitement, she called the doctor: "Doctor, please come at once. My husband's temperature is 136 degrees!" she exclaimed.

The doctor replied, "Madam, the case is beyond my skill. Send for the fire engine." *Link*

SAY THAT AGAIN

A father grew bored reading the same book to his little boy each night and tried a different volume. The child objected: "What did you bring that book I don't want to be read to out of up for?"

Charlton Laird, The Miracle of Language (World)

TOO GOOD FOR A PASSPORT

Two radiologists examined an X-ray photograph.
"Good photo," said one.
"Fairly good," the other agreed, "but it flatters the left lung a little."

AN IDEA

A woman seeking free advice asked a farmer what would be good to plant in a spot that gets very little rain, has too much sun, clay soil and is over a ledge of rock.

"How about a nice flagpole?" replied the farmer.

LABOR PROBLEMS

Impatient customer: "Look, Miss, I only get an hour for lunch!"

Waitress, hurrying by: "I can't discuss labor problems with you now."

FLOOR, PLEASE

Elevator girl: "This is your floor, son."
Boy: "Don't call me son; you're not my mother."
Elevator girl: "I may not be, but I brought you up."

UNUSUAL CASE

Gossip: "What does your husband do for a living?"
Wife: "Well, he has his own business and actually spends all his time minding it."

ONE BAD EXPERIENCE

Lady of the house: "Have you ever been offered work?"
Traveling Idler: "Only once, madam. Aside from that I've met with nothing but kindness."

A COMPACT CAR

An alarmed motorist stopped hurriedly when he saw a young man standing beside an overturned small sports car. "Anybody hurt in the accident?" he inquired.

"There wasn't any accident," replied the young man calmly; "I'm changing a tire."

THE WRONG ANSWER

Little Nellie, a 6-year-old, complained, "Mother, I've got a stomach ache."

"That's because your stomach is empty," the mother replied. "You would feel better if you had something in it."

That afternoon the minister called, and in conversation remarked that he had been suffering all day with a severe headache.

Little Nellie was alert. "That's because it's empty," she said. "You'd feel better if you had something in it."

DRAFTY

Seeing the sheriff, who had been sent by the landlord to serve a summons for past-due rent, coming down the garden path, Jones barred and locked his door, and prepared to hold the fort at all costs.

The sheriff knocked twice, and when there was no response, he pushed the summons under the door.

Immediately Jones blew it back outside with a bellows.

Again the sheriff pushed it under, and again Jones sent it back.

This happened several times until the sheriff finally picked up the summons and said to his deputy: "Come on, let's take this back to the landlord. I wouldn't pay any rent, either, if I had to live in a drafty old house like this."

NO WAY HOME

"Vote for me," boomed the youthful politician in the village hall, "and I'll give you better roads, safer roads; what's more, we'll give you one-way streets."

"That ain't no good 'ere," interrupted a villager with a grin. "We've only got one street—'ow are we goin' to get back 'ome?"   *Tit-Bits, London*

SURPRISED

Little Mary was much surprised when she received a half dollar on her fifth birthday. She kept it in her hands constantly, and finally sat down on a stool, looking intently at the coin.

Her mother said, "Mary, what are you going to do with your half dollar?"

"I'll take it with me to Sunday School," said Mary promptly.

"I guess you want to show it to your teacher," suggested mother.

"Oh, no!" declared Mary; "I'm going to give it to God. I know He will be as surprised as I am to get something besides pennies!"   *Grit*

COULDN'T HELP IT

A fellow stopped for traveling at 70 miles an hour told the policeman: "I can't understand it. I must have had a 40-mile-an-hour tail wind."   *Dublin Opinion*

FIVE DAY WEEK

Robinson Crusoe had leisurely week-ends, yet all was neat and tidy; because—at least the story goes—his work was done by Friday!

POISONED WATERMELON

A Georgia farmer put this sign in front of his watermelon patch:

ONE WATERMELON IN THIS PATCH HAS BEEN POISONED

The next morning the sign had been changed to:

TWO WATERMELONS IN THIS PATCH HAVE BEEN POISONED

MONEY

Money isn't everything. There are greater things in life, if only you can think of them, and then convince your wife!

E. L. Brooks

IS THAT ALL

First Freshman: "I hear you got thrown out of school for calling the dean a fish."

Second Freshman: "I didn't call him a fish. I just said, 'That's our dean,' real fast."

NO NOVELTY

A lecturer was giving a talk before a women's club on life in Egypt, past and present. He mentioned how careless some of the Egyptians were toward their wives. "Why, it is no novelty at all," he said, "to see a woman and a donkey hitched together over there."

"Come to think of it," volunteered a voice from the rear, "it's no novelty in this country either."   *Country Gentleman*

FORECASTING

The class of 6th-graders was discussing various types of prophets and soothsayers. Someone mentioned fortune tellers who gaze into crystal balls, and another said he had seen the tent of a palmist at the country fair. The teacher added that some who try to foretell their customers' future do it with cards.

"That's what my mother does," chirped an excited pupil. "She looks at my report card and tells me what my father is going to do to me when he sees it!"

Marie Fraser, Indiana Teacher

NO USE

"If you can spare me a moment, sir," said the brisk book agent, "I will show you how to earn twice as much money as you are now getting."

Slowly the downtrodden householder shook his head. "Tain't no use," he declared. "I'm doin' that already."

PLENTY HOPI

A tourist had visited an Indian reservation to buy curios, and was talking to an Indian chief. The tourist asked about the Indian's family, and was amazed when the chief said that he had 14 children.

"Well," said the tourist, "with a family that large, don't you have an endless stream of arguments?"

"Oh, no," the Indian replied. "We're just one big Hopi family."

INSPIRATION

Newton, sitting on a wall, watched an autumn apple fall, and found that gravity brought apples to the ground.

Watt, observing someone's kettle boiling near the chimney settle, designed a patent engine that amazed mankind.

I have looked at apples falling and kettles boiling. If I could only think like that!

SHARING SMILES

I had a friendly smile; I gave that smile away. The milkman and the postman seemed glad of it each day. I took it to the shop, I had it on the street; I gave it without thinking to all I chanced to meet. I gave my smile away, as thoughtless as could be; and every time I gave it, my smile came back to me.

Sunshine Magazine

EVEN WORSE HERE

An American and a Dutchman were talking. "What does your flag look like?" asked the American. "It has 3 stripes," replied the Dutchman, "red, white and blue. We say they have a connection with our taxes: we get red when we talk about them, white when we get our tax bills, and we pay 'til we're blue in the face."

"That's just how it is here," commented the American, "only we see stars, too." *R & R Magazine*

SERVING TWO WAYS

Mrs. Sheffield to new maid: "Can you serve company?"
Maid: "Yes, mum—both ways."
Mrs. Sheffield: "What do you mean—both ways?"
Maid: "So's they'll come back, or so's they'll stay away!"

OF COURSE

Teacher: "This essay on 'Our Dog' is word for word the same as your brother's."
Johnny: "Yes'm, I know. It's the same dog."

BE CAREFUL!

A Texan was trying to impress on a Bostonian the valor of the heroes of the Alamo. "I'll bet you never had anything so brave around Boston," said the Texan.

"Did you ever hear of Paul Revere?" asked the Bostonian.

"Paul Revere?" said the Texan, "Isn't he the guy who ran for help?"

A GRUDGE

A visitor from across the mountain leaned on the rail fence, watching his old friend plow. "I don't like to butt in," he finally said, "but you could save yourself a lot of work by saying 'gee' and 'haw' to that mule instead of just tuggin' on them lines."

The old timer pulled a big handkerchief from his pocket and mopped his brow. "Yep, I know that," he agreed, "but this mule kicked me 6 years ago, and I ain't spoke to him since."

IS THAT CLEAR?

A rabbit and a lion entered a restaurant and parked themselves at the counter. "One head of lettuce," ordered the rabbit. "No dressing."

The waiter pointed to the lion. "What'll your friend have?" he asked.

"Nothing."

"What's the matter? Isn't he hungry?"

The rabbit regarded him squarely in the eye. "Look," he said, "if this lion was hungry, do you think I'd be sitting here?"

Tit-Bits, London

YOU CERTAINLY DO

One thing about moving frequently—you may not have many good friends—but you end up with curtains that will fit almost any kind of window.   *Richmond Times-Dispatch*

A COLD CUT

"I seem to be a rose between two thorns," remarked Miss Prettygirl as she seated herself between two men at a football game.

"I'd say it's more like a tongue sandwich," retorted one of the men.

CAREFUL PLANNING

A man motoring thru a rural village stopped at a country store for cigaretes. On the wall was a sign: "This store will be closed Aug. 23 on account of the weather." As it was only Aug. 15 the man asked the proprietor how he could know what the weather would be so far in advance. "Well," said the proprietor, "if she rains light, I'm going fishing. If she rains heavy, I'm going to stay home and work on my tackle."

"But how do you know it's going to rain?" asked the man.

"Don't care if it rains or not," explained the proprietor, "if it's sunny I'll go fishing or work on my tackle anyway. All depends on the weather."   *Indiana Conservation*

PLAYING THREE ROLES

Best vacation story of the Midwest had to do with the Oklahoma woman who was, of necessity, chatting with members of the Texas elite at a Colorado resort. They were going on about their butlers, their chauffeurs and their 2nd maids until she stopped them cold with the announcement that her husband had given a 3-weeks all-expense vacation in the mountains to their cook, their cleaning woman and their gardener. Nor did she find it necessary to explain further that she was all three.

Shawnee (Okla.) News-Star

IT'S POSSIBLE

An old bachelor surprised his friends and married. A few months later the bridegroom was visiting among his former companions when one of them asked: "John, tell us about this marryin' business. Jes' what kind of a match did you make?"

"Well," John replied, "I didn't do as well as I expected." He paused and thought a moment. "And to tell you the truth, I don't think she did, either."   *Arkansas Baptist*

THOUGHTFUL

The young woman, a new driver, entered the police station, and walked up to the sergeant's desk. From her purse she produced a parking ticket and said, "Did one of your men lose this? I found it on my windshield!"

THE SINGING VACATION

"We decided to spend our vacation right here in town this summer," reported our next-door neighbor. "And that happy noise you hear is the eight hundred dollars singing in our bank account."

PITY THE PROOFREADER

Very few Americans fail to thrill to the majestic strains of the national anthem, but consider the proofreader when listening to its rendition by the copyholder:

"Begin quote capital o say comma can you see comma by the

dawn apostrophe s early light comma capital w what so proudly we hailed at the twilight apostrophe s last gleaming interrogation point capital w whose broad stripes and bright stars comma through the perilous fight comma capital o apostrophe er the ramparts we watched comma were so gallantly streaming exclamation point end quote."   *Kalends*

TOO MUCH UPKEEP

To keep up with the Joneses is sheer futility, for while I'm keeping up with them, they're keeping up with me. I cannot keep on keeping up—I'm sunk in now so deep, I'm going to let the Joneses have the keeping up to keep!

EXPENSIVE

The teen-ager sent his girl friend her first orchid with this note: "With all my love and most of my allowance."

RARE

Sign seen in a department store window: "Wonderful bargains in shirts for men with sixteen and seventeen necks."

THE OTHER SIDE

There's a bright side to everything. For every man who is saddened by the thought that he can't take it with him, at least 20 relatives are made happy.   *Wooden Barrel*

THESE EDUCATED YOUNGSTERS

Educators insist that the "crazy" answers that high-school students sometimes give to examination questions are not an indication of deliberate facetiousness—but it seems hard to believe. At any rate, here are a few comments from test papers:

Many Southern parents employed tooters for their children.

The man tried in vain, and was successful.

Shakespeare expressed in his play through the characters that something you gain through dishonesty you loose easily, as MacBeth lost his head in the end.

Typhoid fever can be prevented by facination.

The teacher must be dressed simple. She should wear a commanding look on her countenance.

MacBeth is a typical husband, courageous and strong when away from home.

Question—Name three Greek educators and tell what each one taught. Answer—Socrates, Plato and Aristotle. Socrates taught Plato, and Plato taught Aristotle.

CHOICE

A friend of mine has read all the books on how to deal with children. For example, he'd ask, "What do you want to do first, pick up your toys or hang up your clothes?"

But the 5-year-old soon showed how well he had learned the trick. One day in the toy store, he halted before a display, looked up and demanded of his daddy, "Which one are you going to get me, the scooter or the wagon?"

NATURALLY

It was a quaint expression of a human quality when a good subscriber to her hometown newspaper wrote to the editor as follows: "My sister and I aren't exactly lonely away out here in the country. We've got each other to talk to, but we need another woman to talk about."

WRITING IS EASY

Webster has the words, and I pick them up from where they lie; here a word and there a word—it's so easy, 'tis absurd. I merely 'range them in a row; Webster's done the work, you know. Word follows word, till, inch by inch, I have a column —what a cinch! I take the words that Webster penned and merely lay them end to end.   *Don Marquis*

DANGEROUS TALK

A young midshipman reported to the commanding officer of a battleship for duty. The officer was a gruff old sailor who had worked his way up thru the years. He sized the young man up with anything but a friendly air and said, "Well, I suppose that as usual, they've sent the fool of the family to sea."

"Oh, no, sir," replied the midshipman, candidly, "they've changed all that since your time, sir."   *Link*

WE SUSPECTED THIS

Golf is what letter-carrying, ditch-digging, and carpet-beating would be if those three tasks were to be performed the same afternoon.

HELP

A man, upon arrival of a new heir in his household, placed two cigar boxes on his desk. One box was full of cigars, and bore a sign reading: "It's a girl! Help yourself!" The next cigar box was empty. The accompanying sign read: "It's the 6th one. Help me! All donations gratefully received."

WHAT A FUTURE

Michael had taken a strong dislike to kindergarten. All persuasion failed and finally his mother told him firmly that he would have to go. "All right," retorted Michael, "if you want me to grow up into a bead-stringer, I'll go."

AREN'T WE ALL?

The preacher of a small church in a remote section of the country once preached a funeral service for one of the local mountaineers and he explained the deceased's position in the community thusly:

"Now, he wasn't what you call a good man, because he never gave his heart to the Lord; but he was what you'd call a respected sinner."

THAT'S GOOD ENOUGH

Lad in the 4th grade who can't seem to get the hang of long division left all the answer spaces blank on a recent test paper but printed in neat, square letters across the bottom of the sheet, "I can spell chrysanthemum."   *New Yorker*

IS THAT CLEAR?

A lady with definite ideas was explaining her requirements to the shoe clerk. ". . . and," she concluded, "the shoes must have low heels."

The clerk was a bit confused. "And you wish these to wear with what, madam?" he asked.

"Well," said the matron with an air of finality, "I want them to wear with a short, elderly business man."

IS THAT FAIR?

Registration officer: "Your name, please?"

Spinster: "Matilda Brown."

Officer: "Age?"

Spinster: "Have the Misses Hill, next door, given you their ages?"

Officer: "No."

Spinster: "Well, then, I'm the same age as they."

Officer: "That will do." Proceeding to fill in the form, he murmured: "M. Brown, as old as the hills."

NEW JOB

A dear old lady inquired of a sailor: "What rank did you hold when you were in the navy?"

Sailor: "Ship's optician, lady."

Old lady: "I didn't know there was such a rank. What did you do?"

Sailor: "I scraped the eyes out of the potatoes."

LOST

A man and his wife, hiking in the woods, suddenly realized they had lost their way. Said the husband: "I wish Emily Post were here with us—I think we took the wrong fork."

Hoard's Dairyman

THE BOSS

Two husbands were discussing their status at home. Said one:

"I am the boss in my house. Last night, for example, there was no hot water when I wanted some, so I raised the roof. And, believe me, I got lots of hot water—in a hurry."

Then, after a pause, he added: "I hate to wash dishes in cold water."

Capper's Weekly

ENGLISH AS SHE IS SPOKE

Englishman to American: "What's that noise I 'ear this time of night?"

American: "Why, that's an owl."

Englishman: "Of course it is, but 'oo's 'owling?"

EASY CREDIT

Today's finance: The man had barely paid off his mortgage on the house when he mortgaged it again to buy a car, and not too long after borrowed money to build a garage. His banker hesitated and said, "If I do make this new loan how will you buy gas for the car?"

"It seems to me," the man replied curtly, "that a fellow who owns a large house, a car and garage should be able to get credit for gas."

DON'T KNOW YET

Mrs. White was taken suddenly ill in the night, and a new doctor was called.

After a look at the patient, the doctor stepped outside the sick room to ask Mr. White for a corkscrew. Given the tool, he disappeared but several minutes later was back, demanding a pair of pliers.

Again he disappeared into the room of the moaning patient, only to call out again, "A chisel and a mallet, quickly."

White could stand it no longer. "What is her trouble, doctor?"

"Don't know yet," was the reply. "Can't get my instrument bag open."   *School Activities*

FREE?

A foreigner in Moscow approached a taxicab and asked the driver: "Are you free?"

"No," he said, "I'm a people's democrat."

Ernie Hill, Scripps-Howard Newspapers

MISTAKE

The housewife was exasperated when the plumber finally rang and inquired about the stopped-up laundry tubs.

"It's about time you showed up," she snapped. "I phoned you 5 days ago, on the 10th."

"I guess I must have the wrong house," said the plumber starting to leave. "The party I'm looking for phoned 10 days ago, on the 5th."

VERY USEFUL

A motorist stopped to talk with a farmer erecting a small building. "Whatcha building?" he asked.

"Wal, I tell ya," said the farmer; "if I cin rent it after it's up, it's a rustic cottage, but if'n I cain't, it's a cowshed."

Capper's Weekly

EVERYTHING

A movie actress was applying for a visa. She came to the blank: "Single—Married—Divorced—." She hesitated a moment, then wrote: "Yes."

SIGNS OF AGE

When you turn to the obituaries before the sports news—when you choose a crowded escalator instead of the empty stairs—when you realize how short your arms are getting because you can't tell the 5's, 6's, 8's and 9's apart in the telephone book—when a party is spoiled because you think how awful you will feel tomorrow.   *Executives' Digest*

NOT TOO YOUNG, PLEASE

Therapy treatments had been recommended for an elderly lady. To dispel her nervousness, the doctor told her: "Why a few weeks of this and you'll be 10 years younger."

"Oh, dear," wailed the old lady, "it won't affect my pension, will it?"

COSTLY TO PRODUCE

"It's a genuine antique, sir."

"But you are asking a high price for it."

"Well, sir, look how wages and the cost of materials have gone up."

NO FUN

Jimmy needed a playmate. Grandpa said if Jimmy would stop crying, he would play Indians with him.

Jimmy sobbed even harder, "B-b-but it won't be any fun. You're already scalped." *Senior Scholastic*

PRECISE

A teen-age girl decided to take her brother to a movie on his 12th birthday. Arriving at the box office, she put down the price of two tickets.

"How old is the boy?" asked the ticket-seller suspiciously.

"Well," the girl said, "this is his 12th birthday—but he wasn't born until late in the afternoon."

JUST A CONSUMER

I think that I shall never be a national celebrity. Of that there seems to be small hope—I'll never rise to praise a soap. My fame will never be so great that I'll be advertising bait. No one will ever pay me cash for praising cans of succotash. No advertiser seems to care, whatever I put on my hair.

For this I am not great enough—I'm just the chap who buys the stuff. *Scrapbook*

FIRST SPEECH

The toastmaster rose and with a flourish, introduced the Mayor of a small English town thus: "We welcome His Worship the Mayor as a speaker tonight. This will, in fact, be his 1st speech since his recent marriage." *Public Service, London*

IT ISN'T?

A golfer, after a particularly brutal session in a sand trap, sought to relieve the uncomfortable silence by cheerily declaring to his caddy: "Golf's a funny game." " 'Tain't meant to be," the boy replied.

NOT SO LOUD

A tough Army sergeant entered the barracks where a group of draftees had spent their first night, switched on the lights and bellowed: "All right, you guys! It's 4 o'clock!"

"Four o'clock!" one draftee gasped. "Man, you better get to bed. We got a big day tomorrow."

IS THERE ANY OTHER WAY?

The lady was lucky enough to find a parking space right where she wanted to shop. She backed in until she hit the car in back of her with a loud bang. Then she pulled forward and smacked into the car ahead. This resounding crash drew the attention of the policeman at the corner.

Noticing that he was watching her, the lady called cheerfully, "Did I park all right, Officer?"

"Yes, lady," he answered, "but do you always park by ear?"

THAT WILL CURE HIM

Hubby: "Janet, when I see you in that hat I laugh."
Wife: "Good! I'll put it on when the bill comes in."

AN AMATEUR

Friend: "So you were asked for an opinion of that amateur's playing. What do you think of it?"

Master musician: "He plays in the true spirit of Christian charity."

Friend: "What do you mean?"

Master musician: "His right hand does not know what his left hand is doing."

SURPRISE!

Of all the sad surprises, there's nothing to compare with treading in the darkness on a step that wasn't there.

HE HURRIED

"I wasn't born in a log cabin," declared the candidate, "but my folks moved into one as soon as they could afford it."

Anderson (S. C.) Independent

SING CLEARLY, PLEASE

When singing "God Bless America," a little four-year-old sang it this way: "Stand beside her, and guide her, through the night with a light from a bulb."

WESTERN UPLIFT

Our neighbor is not so sure about the effects of TV Westerns upon young minds.

When he found his young sons emulating a cowboy as he drank, he gave the lads a long lecture on the evils of drinking.

The lesson apparently was effective because, a few days later, his youngest son produced a drawing of a cowboy in a tavern and, when he showed it to his father, he explained quickly: "Don't worry about this cowboy. He didn't go into the tavern to drink anything—just to shoot a man."

AT LAST

A clerk was handed a pay envelope which, through error, contained a blank check.

The astonished clerk looked at it and moaned: "Just what I knew would happen eventually! My deductions have at last caught up with my salary!"

DON'T LOOK BACK

The Sunday School teacher was describing how Lot's wife looked back and turned into a pillar of salt.

Little Johnny was much interested. "My mother looked back once, while she was driving," he explained, "and—and—she turned into a telephone pole!"

BRAGGING

He's like so many men I know who brag and bluster, rant and shout, and beat their manly chests without a single thing to brag about.

A BAD SITUATION

It's hard to lose the girl you love when your heart is full of hope. But it's harder still to lose the towel when your eyes are full of soap.   *Seydell Quarterly*

FRIGHTENING

Accountant, to fellow employee: "For a minute this deficit had me worried. I forgot that I was working for the Government."

SALESMANSHIP

"Grandma, were you a little girl like me once?"

"Yes, dear."

"Then I suppose you know how it feels to get ice cream cones when you don't expect them."

A BOY'S ESSAY ON ANATOMY

Your head is kind of round and hard, and your branes are in it and your hair on it. Your face is the front of your head where you eat and make faces. Your neck is what keeps your head out of your collar. It's hard to keep clean.

Your shoulders are sort of shelfs where you hook your suspenders on them. Your stummick is something that if you do not eat often enough it hurts, and spinage don't help it none.

Your spine is a long bone in your back that keeps you from folding up. Your back is always behind you no matter how quick you turn around.

Your arms you got to have to pitch with, and so you can reach the butter. Your fingers stick out of your hand so you can throw a curve, and add up rithmatick.

Your legs is what if you have not got two of you cannot get to first base, neither can your sister. Your feet are what you run on. Your toes are what always gets stubbed.

And that's all there is of you except what's inside and I never saw it.

FROM DEVOTED SON

"Dear Dad: Let me hear from you more often, even if it's only five or ten."

BE CAREFUL

The talkative lady was telling her husband about the bad manners of a recent visitor. "If that woman yawned once, Albert, while I was talking, she yawned a dozen times!"

"Maybe she wasn't yawning, dear," said the husband; "maybe she was trying to say something."

HE COULDN'T AFFORD TO LEAVE

A soldier who lost his rifle was reprimanded by his captain and told he would have to pay for it.

"Sir," gulped the soldier, "suppose I lost a tank—surely I would not have to pay for that!"

"Yes, you would, too," bellowed the captain, "even if it took the rest of your life."

"Well," said the soldier, "now I know why the captain goes down with his ship."

THAT'S ALL

"What flavors of ice cream do you have?" inquired the customer.

"Vanilla, strawberry, and chocolate," answered the waitress in a hoarse whisper.

Trying to be sympathetic, the customer asked, "Do you have laryngitis?"

"No," replied the waitress with an effort, "just vanilla, strawberry, and chocolate."

GOOD ADVICE

An insurance claim agent was teaching his wife to drive, when the brakes suddenly failed on a steep downhill grade.

"I can't stop," she shrilled. "What shall I do?"

"Brace yourself," advised her husband, "and try to hit something cheap." *The Co-Operator*

WHICH ONE

Employer, interviewing prospective secretary: "How's your spelling? Let me hear you spell Mississippi."

Secretary (stalling): "The river or the state?"

FIRST MAN

"Who was the first man?" asked the teacher of Billy.

"George Washington was the first man. He was first in war, first in peace, and first in the hearts of his countrymen."

"Oh, no," said the teacher, "Adam was the first man."

"Oh, well, Teacher, if you want to bring foreigners in on it, you may be right," conceded Billy.

IS THAT CLEAR

Said the little girl, "What is the mortar board I hear mentioned so often?"

"I'll try to explain," said the teacher, "although it is a slightly complicated matter. A mortar board carried by a builder often has cement on top, and worn by a college professor often has concrete underneath."

FRANKLY

Quin Ryan tells this story: When a little boy's mother asked him whom he loved the most he replied: "Well, I like you best, and then comes daddy, and teacher last—but in between come a lot of dogs."

OF COURSE

A fellow was walking his long-haired dachshund and he met a friend who said "What a funny animal! How do you tell his head from his tail?"

"It's very simple," the dog's owner replied. "You pull its tail and if it bites you, you know it was his head."

SHUT YOUR EYES

Jimmy: "Dad, can you sign your name with your eyes shut?"

Dad: "Certainly."

Jimmy: "Well, then, shut your eyes and sign my report card."

TO THE HEAD OF THE CLASS

"Willie," asked the teacher of the new pupil, "do you know your alphabet?"

"Yessum," answered Willie.

"Well, then," continued the teacher, "what letter comes after A?"

"All of 'em," was Willie's reply.

PRODIGIES

Two first-graders stood talking and looking skyward when a huge jet flew over. "Just look at that," said the first one. "It's a BX-50."

"No, it isn't—it's a BX-41," said the other, "and it's not going more than 750 miles an hour because it didn't break the sound barrier."

The first boy agreed on this point and said, "It's really quite amazing the pressure that develops on those planes when they go into a dive—almost 1200 pounds per square inch."

Just then, the school bell rang and all the kids started back to class rooms. The first boy sighed and said, "Oh, well . . . let's go back in and string those colored beads again."

UNDERPRIVILEGED

The latest class of underprivileged children are those whose parents own two cars but no speedboat.

HELPFUL LAUNDRY

From Milwaukee comes the report that a lady called her laundry to complain that she had received, in her bundle, six men's sox.

"I'm not even married!" the lady customer declared.

"We're sorry," answered the helpful girl at the laundry. "We'll send a man out right away."

THAT'S DIFFERENT

The boss: "I wish you wouldn't sing when you are working."
The helper: "I wasn't working, sir; I was just singing."

TOUGH NEIGHBORHOOD

Some men were discussing the tough neighborhoods in which they'd grown up.

"Listen," said one, "my neighborhood was so tough that any cat there with a tail was a tourist."

EMPTY HANDED

Inviting a friend to his wedding anniversary, the man explained: "We're on the seventh floor, apartment 7D. Just touch the button with your elbow."

"And why should I use my elbow?"

"Well, for goodness sake, you're not coming emptyhanded, are you?"

ONE POINT OF VIEW

Two youngsters had strayed away from their mother in a department store and were riding up and down the crowded elevators. Suddenly the boy noticed that his ice cream cone was dripping and wiped it against the back of a woman's mink coat.

"For goodness sake, Jimmy, watch yourself," whispered his sister. "You're getting fur all over your ice cream."

ANOTHER ONE ABOUT TEXAS

Robert Q. Lewis tells about the Texan whose car went out of control and he hit a dozen cars before he could stop. Luckily, it happened in his own garage.

ACHIEVEMENT

Like most 6-year-olds, Peter abhorred washing, and came to the dinner table one evening with elbows black as pitch. Sent back to the bathroom for repairs, he dawdled there so long that his mother called, "Are you coming, Peter? Elbows clean yet?"

"Not clean," he called back triumphantly, "but I got them to match."

IT TAKES TIME

Two small boys put their hands side by side.
"Hah! Mine's dirtier'n yours," said one.
"Well," said the other, "you're a year older'n me."

BE CAREFUL

A modern mother and her young son were shopping in a supermarket. The child, trying to be helpful, picked up a package and brought it to her.

"Oh, no, honey!" protested the mother. "Go put it back. You have to cook that!"

PERFECTLY CLEAR

A bookseller had a statement for a book curtly returned to him with this note written across it: "Dear Sir: I never ordered this beastly book. If I did, you didn't send it. If you sent it, I never got it. If I got it, I paid for it. If I didn't, I won't!"

ANCESTORS

Lives of ancestors remind us, we give photos to our kin; and, departing, leave behind us relatives who point and grin.
                    Louisville Courier-Journal Magazine

NEW COOK

A newly married man found his wife sitting stock still in the kitchen. She was following a recipe which said, "Don't stir for fifteen minutes."

LONG TIME NO SEE

Mr. Jones stared in a puzzled way at Mr. Clark, to whom he had just been introduced. "You look like a man I've seen somewhere, Mr. Clark," he said. "Your face seems familiar. A funny thing about it is that I remember I formed a strong prejudice against the man who looks like you—but I'm sure we never met."

Mr. Clark laughed. "I'm the man," he answered, "and I know why you formed the prejudice. I passed the contribution plate for 2 years in the church you attended.   *Scholastic Teacher*

OF COURSE

An Irishman was trying to enlist in the army. He said he was 41 whereas the age limit was 38. But the recruiting sergeant thought the Irishman would make a good soldier and told him to go out and think about the age matter and return. In an hour the Irishman was back.

"Well, how old are you now?" asked the sergeant.

"Sure, it's 38 I am; it's me old mither who is 41."

SAME DECISION

Two acquaintances met outside a polling place during a recent election and both started to talk about the candidates up for election. Finally they came to several men who were listed as candidates for the office of mayor.

"Ben," remarked one voter, "I don't want to vote for any of these men. Why, I don't know a one of them."

"I'm in the same position, Bill," replied the other sadly. "I know them all."

ANOTHER VIEW

India is an old nation but a young republic. We, in comparison, are a young nation but an old republic.

This truth is pointed up in the story of a U. S. tourist who visited an Indian village. "Have you ever heard of America?" he asked an old peasant.

The Indian scratched his head. "America?" he replied. "Oh, I guess you mean the country Columbus found when he was looking for India."   *Senior Scholastic*

WHAT GOT HIM

Some years ago, the *New Yorker* presented a cartoon which shows two young theological students walking within the cloistered walls of the seminary. One of the students has a baffled expression on his countenance, and is remarking to the other: "What gets me about this place is that they want you to love people you don't even like!"

Robert E. Fitch, The New Leader

CHAPTER V

INSPIRING ILLUSTRATIONS AND IDEAS

HOW TO LIVE

To awaken each morning with a smile brightening my face;
to greet the day with reverence for the opportunities it contains; to approach my work with a clean mind; to hold ever
before me, even in the doing of little things, the ultimate purpose toward which I am working; to meet men and women
with laughter on my lips and love in my heart; to be gentle,
kind, and courteous through all the hours; to approach the
night with weariness that ever woos sleep and the joy that
comes from work well done—this is how I desire to waste
wisely my days.   *Thomas Dekker*

A WISE MAN

He is a wise man who does not grieve for the things which he
has not, but rejoices for those which he has.   *Epictetus*

WHAT YOU HAVE

Let not your mind run on what you lack as much as on what
you have already. Of the things you have, select the best; and
then reflect how eagerly they would have been sought if you
did not have them.   *Marcus Aurelius*

WE HAVE THE MEANS

God gives every bird its food, but He does not throw it into
the nest. He does not unearth the good that the earth contains,
but He puts it in our way, and gives us the means of getting it
ourselves.   *J. G. Holland*

MONEY

It's good to have money and the things that money can buy,
but it's good, too, to check up once in a while and make sure
you haven't lost the things that money can't buy.

George Horace Lorimer

93

NOW IS THE TIME

Men spend their lives in anticipation, in determining to vastly happy at some period or other, when they have time. the present time has one advantage over every other: it is own. *Charles C. Colto*

FAITH

Without faith a man can do nothing; with it all things possible. *Sir William Osler*

ONE NIGHT IN A THOUSAND YEARS

If the stars should appear one night in a thousand years, how men would believe and adore, and preserve for many genera-tions the remembrance of the City of God which had been shown! But every night come out these envoys of beauty, and light the universe with their admonishing smile. . . .
Ralph Waldo Emerson

SLEEP IN PEACE

Have courage for the great sorrows of life and patience for the small ones; and when you have laboriously accomplished your daily task, go to sleep in peace. God is awake.
Victor Hugo

THE DAWN

For half a century I have been writing my thoughts in prose and in verse—history, philosophy, drama, romance, tradition, satire, ode, and song. I have tried all. But I feel I have not said the thousandth part of what is in me. When I go down to the grave I can say, like many others, "I have finished my day's work!" But I cannot say, "I have finished my life." My day's work will begin again the next morning. The tomb is not a blind alley; it is a thoroughfare. It closes on the twilight, it opens on the dawn. *Victor Hugo*

FAITH

Where faith is there is courage, there is fortitude, there is steadfastness and strength. . . .

Faith bestows that sublime courage that rises superior to the troubles and disappointments of life, that acknowledges no defeat except as a step to victory; that is strong to endure, patient to wait, and energetic to struggle. . . . Light up, then, the lamp of faith in your heart. . . . It will lead you safely through the mists of doubt and the black darkness of despair; along the narrow, thorny ways of sickness and sorrow, and over the treacherous places of temptation and uncertainty.

James Allen

ACCEPTANCE

Be willing to have it so. Acceptance of what has happened is the first step to overcoming the consequences of any misfortune.

William James

HAVE WE FORGOTTEN?

And have we now forgotten that powerful Friend? Or do we imagine we no longer need His assistance? I have lived a long time; and the longer I live, the more convincing proofs I see of this truth: that God governs in the affairs of men. And if a sparrow cannot fall to the ground without His notice, is it probable that an empire can rise without His aid?

Benjamin Franklin

STUNNED BY THE TEMPEST

We shall steer safely through every storm, so long as our heart is right, our intention fervent, our courage steadfast, and our trust fixed on God. If at times we are somewhat stunned by the tempest, never fear. Let us take breath, and go on fresh.

Francis de Sales

HIS PROGRAM

My program is work, for man was designed for labor. "Thou shalt live by the sweat of thy brow" was written centuries ago and the immutable destiny of man will never change. What each man has to do is to try to progress in his profession, to strive for constant improvement so as to become effective and skillful in whatever career he has chosen and to attain superiority by the cultivation of his natural gifts and by his devotion to work. That is the path I have laid out for myself. All the rest is mere dreaming or speculation.   *Jean Francois Millet*

WAKING UP SOMEBODY

Perseverance is a great element of success. If you only knock long enough and loud enough at the gate, you are sure to wake up somebody.   *Henry Wadsworth Longfellow*

FAITH

Our friend and we were invited abroad on a party of pleasure, which is to last forever. His chair was ready first, and he is gone before us. We could not all conveniently start together; and why should you and I be grieved at this, since we are soon to follow, and know where to find him.   *Benjamin Franklin*

WHAT CAN I DO?

Our daughter, Kathy, often talks to God following her formal prayers. Usually, she asks for many things. But one night, after her list of requests, she paused and added, "And now, God, what can I do for you?"

The question jolted me. What can she—or I or anyone—do for God?

Certainly, I don't know if we can do anything for Him. But I've decided that one way to serve God is by taking a real and continuing part in church life. For me, there has been no one great inspirational moment. But, over a period of time, my family and I have discovered that church attendance and religious experiences have added new strength to our lives. It's a strength we all need . . . and you won't find it any other way.   *Robert Young, actor*

HAPPINESS AND MISERY

To me there is in happiness an element of self-forgetfulness. You lose yourself in something outside yourself when you are happy; just as when you are desperately miserable you are intensely conscious of yourself, are a solid little lump of ego weighing a ton.   *J. B. Priestley*

LITTLE THINGS

One day in Colorado a great, stalwart tree fell down. It was a sapling when Columbus landed at San Salvador. It had been struck by lightning fourteen times. It had braved storms, defied earthquakes, and bent beneath the fierce onslaughts of mountain torrents. But in the end, tiny beetles killed it. They bored under the bark, dug into its heart, ate away its mighty fibres—and one day down toppled the great king of the forest.

Mutual Moments

SEARCH FOR SECURITY

A family had failed to make a living on a worn-out New England farm. Did they demand government subsidies, checks for crops they didn't raise, high prices for crops to be burned? They would have scorned such things—scorned and feared, for they knew from days under a foreign despot that where government money goes, government control goes too.

No, this family put everything they owned in a wagon, and walked beside it two thousand miles, westward. They did not know what was ahead, but they were determined to keep on going until they found a place of freedom where they could keep their self-respect.

They were English, Scotch, Dutch, Italian, French—people from many places—all, now, Americans. They knew that the only happiness is from self-respect, and the only way to self-respect is to earn your own way, not whine for something for nothing.

Their sons and grandsons started grocery stores, became mechanics, saved their money, and started factories. American machines bought by American thrift made the factories grow.

And that's America. Made by people willing to walk two thousand miles beside a wagon, to find opportunity. If such people are gone, if all we have left are soft weaklings who want to be taken care of, then in truth American manliness is dead, that 2,000-mile walk was wasted, and there is nothing left of America but a hollow shell!

Statement issued by Warner and Swasey, Manufacturers, Cleveland, Ohio. Reprinted with permission in Sunshine Magazine

MOST IMPORTANT

A roving reporter stopped six people on the sidewalks of New York City and asked: "What was the most important happening in history?" Five replies, from two men and three women, were as varied as might be expected:

"The settlement of Jamestown by the English."

"The defeat of the Saracens at Tours."

"The splitting of the atom."

"The defeat of the Japanese."

"The invention of the wheel."

The sixth answer came from a 14-year-old schoolboy: "The birth of Jesus Christ."   *Evangelical Press*

CHRISTMAS

It's Christmas! Let us give thanks to God, who guides our destiny, for the many blessings bestowed on America—free worship, free speech, free press, free ballot, free schools, and free enterprise. As we pay homage to Deity in our churches and in our homes, around the festive board and Christmas tree, let us so value these privileges that we may ever be on the alert to defend our freedom against tyranny. Let us by our actions and deeds give succor and courage to those less fortunate people who suffer aggression and oppression. Let us pray that America forever stand a Christian bulwark before all the world.

From GM Folks, of General Motors Corporation

FAITH

What is faith unless it is to believe what you do not see?

St. Augustine

VICTORY OVER HIMSELF

He who gains a victory over other men is strong; but he who gains a victory over himself is all powerful.   *Lao-tse*

CONFORMITY

If a man does not keep pace with his companions, perhaps it is because he hears a different drummer. Let him keep step to music which he hears, however measured or far away.

Henry David Thoreau

THIS TRUTH ALONE

To love our neighbor as ourself is such a fundamental truth for regulating human society, that by that alone one might determine all the cases in social morality.   *John Locke*

FRIENDSHIP

If a man does not make new acquaintances as he advances through life, he will soon find himself left alone. A man should keep his friendships in constant repair. . . .

To let friendship die away by negligence and silence is certainly not wise. It is voluntarily to throw away one of the greatest comforts of this weary pilgrimage. *Samuel Johnson*

LIFE IS NOW

The greatest gift . . . is the realization that life does not consist either of wallowing in the past or of peering anxiously at the future; and it is appalling to contemplate the great number of often painful steps by which one arrives at a truth so old, so obvious, and so frequently expressed. It is good for one to appreciate that life is now. Whatever it offers, little or much, life is now—this day—this hour.   *Charles Macomb Flandrau*

WORTH REMEMBERING

Nothing in human affairs is worth any great anxiety.
                                                                Plato

THE BEST OF NOW

No longer forward nor behind
I look in hope or fear;
But grateful, take the good I find,
The best of now and here.
                          John Greenleaf Whittier

WHAT WEALTH IS

These things I know: I have planted a garden, so I know what faith is. I have seen poplar trees swaying in the breeze, so I know what grace is. I have listened to birds caroling, so I know what music is.

I have seen a morning without clouds, after showers, so I know what beauty is. I have read a book beside a wood fire, so I know what contentment is. I have seen the miracle of the sunset, so I know what grandeur is.

And because I have perceived all these things, I know what wealth is.   *Capper's Weekly*

A CHARACTER QUIZ

1. If you found a pocketbook with $1,000, would you give it to the owner if no one would ever know you found it?

2. If you could advance yourself by unfair methods, would you do it if no one would ever find out you were unfair?

3. If the bus driver failed to collect your fare, would you voluntarily pay it?

4. If there were no locks on any house, store, or bank, would you take anything if no one would ever find out?

5. If your business partner died, would you pay his relatives their fair share, if you did not have to pay them?

6. If you were an employer trying to hire an efficient, honest, and competent employee, would you hire yourself at your salary?

7. If you are an employer would you like to be working for yourself with the wages, hours, and working conditions you provide?

8. If you are a parent, would you like to be the child of a parent just like you are?

9. If you had your choice, would you like to live in a community with people working in church, civic and community affairs just like you do?

10. If you had to live with someone just like you are for the rest of your life, would you look forward to it as a wonderful opportunity and privilege?   *Herbert V. Prochnow*

DOING NOTHING

A boy from the American Middle West, who had never before seen the ocean, made a trip to the West Coast. As he looked out across the vast Pacific, he stood quiet. "Well," asked a friend, "what do you think of it?"

"It's wonderful," replied the boy, "but I hate to see all that water out there doing nothing."

So it is with scores of people in every community. People who can and won't. People who should and don't. People who take from life and never give. *Wallace Fridy, The Rotarian*

BEAUTIFUL

No adult can possibly be as wise as a happy child can be. Coming home from church services Sunday night, our family paused in the snow for a moment to study the star-gemmed sky. "Goodness!" breathed our Babe, after an appreciative silence. "If heaven is that beautiful on the bottom, just think how wonderful the other side must be!"

Burton Hillis, Better Homes & Gardens

WHY SO HURRIED?

Why should we live with such hurry and waste of life? . . . When we are unhurried and wise, we perceive that only great and worthy things have any permanent and absolute existence, that petty fears and petty pleasures are but the shadow of the reality. *Henry David Thoreau*

THE HIGHEST HAPPINESS

The highest happiness on earth is in marriage. Every man who is happily married is a successful man even if he has failed in everything else. *William Lyon Phelps*

YOU ARE FORTUNATE

It is sad to see so many men and women afraid of growing old. They are in bondage to fear. Many of them, when they find the first gray hair, are alarmed. Now one really ought not to be alarmed when one's hair turns gray; if it turned green or blue, then one ought to see a doctor. But when it turns gray, that simply means there is so much gray matter in the skull there is no longer room for it; it comes out and discolors the hair. Don't be ashamed of your gray hair; wear it proudly, like a flag. You are fortunate, in a world of so many vicissitudes, to have lived long enough to earn it. *William Lyon Phelps*

HOME

God gives all men all earth to love,
    But since man's heart is small,
Ordains for each one spot should prove
    Beloved over all.   *Rudyard Kipling*

DEDICATING OURSELVES

It is given to us, of this generation, to achieve real peace—if not for ourselves, for our children.

It is given to us to reassert the right of man to live as the image of God. To those who say that these unlimited objectives are unthinkable, impossible, let us reply that it is the alternative to them which is unthinkable, impossible for Americans to contemplate. Let us dedicate ourselves to the achievement of these unlimited objectives as boldly and as surely and as confidently as did Columbus and Washington and all the countless millions of Americans, from the Pilgrims to the pioneers, who have proved that in this unconquerably and justifiably optimistic nation nothing undertaken by free men and free women is impossible.   *Robert E. Sherwood*

LOVE YOUR ENEMIES

There is such a destructive reflex action in the soul of a man who allows himself to hate another that it is surprising any sensible person would allow himself to be subjected to it. Hate is a poison which vitiates all character, and brings about the degeneration of personality.

This story was told of General Robert E. Lee: Hearing General Lee speak in the highest terms to President Davis about a certain officer, another officer, greatly astonished, said to him, "General, do you not know that the man of whom you speak so highly to the President is one of your bitterest enemies, and misses no opportunity to malign you?"

"Yes," replied General Lee, "but the President asked my opinion of him; he did not ask for his opinion of me."
          Sunshine Magazine

MASTERING OUR ENVIRONMENT

The first settlers to arrive in the Imperial Valley in southern California found it a vast area of waste land, superheated in the summer and utterly barren and sterile in the winter. But a few courageous souls decided that they would mix a little water with the soil, and today it is the vegetable garden of the nation.

It is true that the Imperial Valley made those pioneers a weathered, bent, hard-bitten company, but those pioneers made the valley a scene of industry and prosperity.

John Wesley rode up and down through the English countryside during the last half of the eighteenth century, his soul touched by the poverty, the drabness, and the ugliness of the village life. One day he hit upon the scheme of distributing flower seeds to the housewives, and offering prizes for the most beautiful gardens, with the result that today the English countryside has the reputation of being the most colorful in the world. One man, almost single-handed, changed the complexion of the rural districts of an entire nation.

Glenn Stewart

THE LORD WAS THEIR SHEPHERD

The first thing they did when they got off ship was to kneel down under the open sky and thank God. That was why they had come here . . . to meet God in the way they thought right.

It was a simple, manly way they had with Him. Each man seeking His presence, reading His Word, listening to His voice, trying to understand His way and to live by it. Each man a free man, responsible to God.

It was not only on Sundays, or in church alone, that they thought of Him, but always and everywhere. They felt that the world was God's house, and they walked reverently in it, and they tried to remember to live by His ways.

So it was that when they wrote a Declaration of Independence, in that fateful moment of making themselves a nation, they called upon Him to behold the justice of what they were about to do.

And when they met to draw up a Constitution, governing how Americans should behave towards each other, they prayed for guidance from the Highest Lawgiver of all.

And from that day to this, when we come together to make a solemn public decision, we take a moment to ask God to make our minds wise, and our hearts good, and our motives pure.

Surely there never was a better country to find God. Out on the open coast, where the ocean stirs forever and ever, always changing and always the same; on the prairies where the grass blows and ripens and dies and is born again; in the wild, high mountains and in the silent desert—everywhere under this wide sky the feeling comes: Some one has been here. Some one has made this beautiful for me. Some one expects me to be worthy of this.

Some one expects me to be worthy . . . Through most of our history we have lived with that faith, and only as long as we believe it, and go on living by it, will we be secure.

Herbert T. Chase

HOPE

I never knew a night so black that light failed to follow in its track. I never knew a storm so gray that it failed to have its clearing day. I never knew such bleak despair that there was not a rift somewhere. I never knew an hour so drear that love could not fill it full of cheer!   *John Kendrick Bangs*

THE WATCHFUL CHRIST OF THE ANDES

The Christ of the Andes statue, standing on the Chile-Argentine boundary line, symbolizes a pledge made by the two countries. As long as the statue stands, it was agreed, there shall be peace and good-will between Argentina and Chile.

But, ironically enough, the statue itself was the cause of what almost resulted in open conflict. When the work was completed, someone pointed out that the Saviour's back was toward Chile. Chileans felt they had been slighted. But while indignation was at its height, a Chilean newspaperman saved the day. In an editorial he explained: "The Argentineans need more watching over than the Chileans."

This satisfied the people. They laughted good-naturedly, and went back to their daily tasks.   *Sunshine Magazine*

CHRISTMAS IN BETHLEHEM

Christmas is observed in Bethlehem on December 25 by both Protestants and Roman Catholics, on January 6 by the Greek Orthodox churches, and on January 18 by the Armenians. The grotto-like "Cave of the Nativity" is in no way comparable to the modern conception of a "stable," but in Biblical times shelters for man and beast were hewn into rocky ledges—thus the stable of Bethlehem. On Christmas Eve members of all denominations assemble to sing carols above the birthplace of the Holy Child, and the sound of the singing is most impressive as it floats through the city, borne by the quiet breezes.

PREPARING FOR TESTS

When one is young and in school, one somehow thinks that someday the time for taking examinations will be over. Now, this is not true at all. We are never done with examinations. All through life they keep coming. Some day you will make your first speech in public, and you will feel that the whole world is examining you, and it may make you nervous.

One test after another will come. For many of them you will not be fully prepared, and you will be inclined to worry a good deal. It is perhaps just as well that we all do worry a little bit. It helps us to do our best. The important thing to remember is that we owe it to ourselves, and to our friends, and to the world, to prepare for the examinations as well as we reasonably can, and then to conduct ourselves during them as honestly and bravely as we can, and not worry about it.

Dwight W. Morrow to his son

WHAT WE DO WITH DESTINY

It is not what destiny does with us, but what we do with destiny that determines what we shall become. When a man is determined, what can stop him?

Cripple him, and you have a Sir Walter Scott : : Put him in a prison cell, and you have a John Bunyan : : Bury him in the snows of Valley Forge, and you have a George Washington : : Have him born in abject poverty, and you have a Lincoln : : Load him with bitter racial prejudice, and you have a Disraeli

: : Stab him with rheumatic pains until for years he cannot sleep without an opiate, and you have a Steinmetz : : Put him in the grease pit of a locomotive roundhouse, and you have a Walter P. Chrysler : : Make him second fiddler in an obscure South American orchestra, and you have a Toscanini.

Our humanity is not our weakness, but our strength. Despite much of the artificiality of life around us, the two greatest words in the English language still are, *"I can!"*

THE GREAT VALUES

To have faith in the dignity and worth of the individual man, to believe that it is better to be governed by persuasion than by coercion, to believe that fraternal goodwill is more worthy than a selfish and contentious spirit, to believe that in the long run all values are inseparable from the love of truth and the disinterested search of it, to believe that knowledge and the power it confers should be used to promote the welfare and happiness of all men . . . these are the values which are affirmed by the traditional ideology; they are the values which men have commonly employed to measure the advance of civilization; the values which men have celebrated in the saints and the sages.

From Carl Becker in Yale Review

ONLY MEN

Not gold, but only men, can make
  A nation great and strong.
Men who, for truth and honor's sake,
  Stand fast, and suffer long.
Brave men, who work while others sleep,
  Who dare while others shy.
They build a nation's pillars deep,
  And lift them to the sky.

Emerson

DOING GREAT WORK

To do great work one must fall in love with his task. Cellini, the goldsmith, pouring his whole soul into his creations, achieved masterpieces, and the love he thus liberated brought him the praise of kings. You've seen the designer of a piece of machinery pat it with pride, as he might pat the head of a son. It is a part of him. He has built his personality into it. That's why it is such a fine machine.

Work that is done in a spirit of love glows with a mystic quality no one can explain. And the worker feels as did Robert Louis Stevenson, who said, "I know what happiness is, for I have done good work."   *The Hoover Sphere*

HOW OLD?

Youth is not entirely a time of life; it is a state of mind. It is not wholly a matter of ripe cheeks, red lips, or supple knees. It is a temper of the will, a quality of the imagination, a vigor of the emotions, a freshness of the deep springs of life. It means a temperamental predominance of courage over timidity, of an appetite for adventure over love of ease.

Nobody grows old by merely living a number of years. People grow old only by deserting their ideals. Years may wrinkle the skin, but to give up interest wrinkles the soul. Worry, doubt, self-distrust, fear and despair . . . these are the long, long years that bow the head and turn the growing spirit back to dust.

Whatever your years, there is in every being's heart the love of wonder, the undaunted challenge of events, the unfailing, childlike appetite for "what next," and the joy and the game of life.

You are as young as your faith, as old as your doubt; as young as your self-confidence, as old as your fear; as young as your hope, as old as your despair. In the central place of your heart, there is a recording chamber; so long as it receives messages of beauty, hope, cheer, and courage, so long you are young. When the wires are all down, and your heart is covered with the snow of pessimism and the ice of cynicism, then—and then only— are you grown old.   *Douglas MacArthur*

ON HIS KNEES

A preacher, while watching a marble cutter at work, exclaimed: "I wish I could deal such clanging blows on stony hearts!" The workman replied: "Maybe you could if you worked like me, on your knees."

"Gib" McMasters, Railroad Evangelist

INNER SIMPLICITY

We have measured success by our products rather than by ourselves. A materialism which over-emphasizes short-term survival detracts from the humanism essential to long-term survival. We must remember that it was not the outer grandeur of the Roman, but the inner simplicity of the Christian that lived thru the ages.   *Charles A. Lindbergh*

CHAPTER VI

QUOTATIONS FROM SERMONS AND SPEECHES

A LIVING PHILOSOPHY

Shortly before his life was taken in Rome, the Apostle Paul wrote a letter to the Philippians containing a challenging philosophy of life. In substance he said, "This one thing I do; forgetting the hardships of the past, and looking to the future, I shall strive to follow the ideals of Christianity."

In these words there are three thoughts which provide a significant living philosophy. They may determine whether life is to be a futile experience or a great adventure.

In the first place, when one says, "This one thing I *do,*" it indicates that he has made an important decision. A positive and unmistakable choice is evident. The ability to make up one's mind—to quit straddling—to decide—is one of the essentials in a vital philosophy of life. It means choosing between the wise and the foolish, the good and the bad, the beautiful and the ugly, the virtues and the vulgarities of life.

Every hour we are confronted by decisions. Of course we will make the right decisions when they are easy. But will we have the courage to make decisions that meet the tests of our religious faith when these decisions are difficult and even unpopular?

Many times decisions are not easy. Albert Schweitzer, living in a hut in Africa for his ideals; Abraham Lincoln carrying on his shoulders the terrible burden of a nation engaged in civil war—these men could testify to the price men pay for courageous decisions. Small minds, lazy minds, weak minds always take the easiest way—always make the easiest decisions.

Life is the sum total of all the decisions one makes. Nothing more—nothing less. There is no such thing as indecision. Life is made up one way or the other. When you fail to decide, you are deciding. Life gets made up. Life gets lived one way or the other.

You will remember the Prodigal Son who said to his father, "Give me now the share of goods that I am to inherit later." The father gave it to him and the young man left for a far country, where he squandered his entire estate. He was destitute. He was hungry. He had no friends. He might have said bitterly, "My father was too indulgent. He was mature. I was a boy. He should not have been so foolish as to give me my estate." But this young man had learned a hard lesson, and he made a great decision. He said, "I will go to my father and say to him 'Father, I was wrong . . . and am no more worthy to be called your son; make me one of your hired servants.'" Of course, his father accepted him, and with that courageous decision, the young man found the life he had lost.

Secondly, when a person says, "This *one* thing I do," he states in unmistakable terms that his life is to have a singleness of purpose. One thing is to have first place in his life.

Many of us would like to be great in some field, but are we really willing by the hardest work, the longest hours and the greatest sacrifice to achieve that ambition? We dilly dally, unwilling to pay the price demanded of pursuing a single great objective. Walt Whitman said, "I was simmering, simmering, simmering: Emerson brought me to a boil." Many of us in life succeed in our goals to where we almost reach the boiling point. Nearly, you see, almost, but not quite.

It takes struggles in life to make strength. It takes fight for principles to make fortitude. It takes crises to give courage. Suffering to make sympathy. Pain to make patience. It takes singleness of purpose to place the highest ideals of one's religious faith first in life.

Finally, then, this is the decision, and this is the single objective in life: to take whatever occupation or profession one may be in—doctor, businessman, farmer, dentist, banker, attorney, teacher, housewife—and to strive each day to live in accordance with the high ideals of one's religious faith. Consider how this living philosophy may be practically applied.

If you demand good government in your city, your state and your country, you will discharge your full responsibilities as a good citizen.

If you demand that crime be in the cell and not in the saddle in your community, you will support honest law enforcement without any personal privileges or exceptions for yourself.

If you demand special advantages, government bonuses, subsidies, and privileges for your business, your union, your city or your state, you will remember that the price of such selfishness is the deterioration of a nation's character.

If you demand freedom of worship for yourself, you will respect the rights of other creeds.

If you demand that the government give you complete economic security, you will not forget that a nation's strength comes when each person first does his best by work and self-denial to stand on his own feet.

If you profess Christianity, you will in a spirit of humility earnestly endeavor to make your own life an inspiring example of its ideals in your home, your business and your community.

You may remember the play "Green Pastures." In that play, Noah said to the Lord, "I ain't very much, but I'm all I've got."

Well, you're all you've got. I'm all I've got. What are we doing with what we've got? Are we striving to attain those ideals of our faith which lead to a great and good life?

Someone may say that this living philosophy is the counsel of perfection. And so it is. As the days and weeks and years of life go by, the person who lives it will be able to say with joy, "I have fought the good fight, I have finished my course, I have kept the faith."

Herbert V. Prochnow, speaking before the Chicago Sunday Evening Club

FIRST THINGS FIRST

For generations (the typical American) has been indoctrinated with heresies—that you can get something for nothing, that peace and security should be in the bargain basement, that technology is science, that skill is reason, that a politician is a statesman, and that the best proof of intelligence is meeting a payroll.

. . . Unless we put first things first; unless we take the measure of our challenge and our shortcomings; unless we push through the fog of complacency and self-deceit that still engulfs us, our troubles will compound and our perils will increase. . . . And we shall have to face the distasteful fact that there is something more important than comfortable family life, a split-level ranchhouse, Social Security and three cars in the garage.   *Adlai Stevenson*

WHO ARE YOU?

Again, a study of the self may give a clue to the sense of lostness in modern man. When Uncle Toby in Laurence Sterne's *Tristram Shandy* was debarking after a trip abroad, a customs official asked him, "Who are you?", to which Uncle Toby replied in true Shandyean manner, "Don't confuse me." This reply, in a facetious vein by a character in fiction, is precisely the response many modern men would give in dead earnest to the same question. For contemporary man is very much confused about who he is, where he is, and whither he is bound. He seems to have lost his bearings. His world has no center, no frame of reference, and he himself is without chart or compass. This lostness is often reflected in our poetry and our drama. The pathetic figure and career of Willie Loman, the little Brooklyn salesman, in Arthur Miller's *The Death of a Salesman,* is a dramatic image of this lostness. After his tragic death, and the funeral is over, his son Biff sums up his father's mixed-up life and its failure in six short words: "He never knew who he was." This is the plight of many today, who do not know who they are, or what it means to be human.

Dr. Robert Worth Frank

A SIGNIFICANT REVOLUTION

In August 1914, there was thunder on the horizon. Thirty-one years later in August 1945, when the terrifying clouds had lifted at Hiroshima, the world had been through two disastrous wars. There were shattered empires and bankrupt nations. There were staggering debts. There was deep weariness and sad disillusion. Millions were dead and millions wandered as destitute refugees on the highways of the world. There were desperate cries in the night as men lost their freedom in the satellite nations. There was an alarming drift to socialism and communism over the world as men and women desperately sought economic security.

Today, civilization continues in political and economic turmoil as the great nations engage in a vast cold war. There are restless tossings of the human spirit as men dream of a more fruitful use of life than to spend their creative energy and labor for mounting armaments and the instruments of destruction. Since 1914, the world has been undergoing one of the most significant political, economic, social and scientific revolutions in the history of man.

Changes of great magnitude are taking place in the American economy, and they present us with critical problems. These changes are certain to have an increasingly profound effect upon the life of every citizen, every business and every institution.

Herbert V. Prochnow

THE STRUGGLE TO ENDURE

In 1787, the fifty-five founders of this Republic of only three million people, met in Philadelphia. They created a new nation with a written Constitution setting forth the rights of free men. To paraphrase a great American, we are now engaged in a world struggle to see whether this nation or any nation so conceived can long endure.   *Herbert V. Prochnow*

THE GOOD OLD DAYS

I remember easily events and conditions of the last 60 years. These years span the time between the horse and buggy age and that of 55,000,000 private automobiles; also, the time between Marconi's primitive experiments and television in the many homes of the U. S.; also the time when the 20th Century Limited was the magnificent train through the local town of my boyhood and its virtual discontinuance because of the competition of aeroplanes. I have some nostalgia for the old days. What could be so thrilling as a ride with grandfather in a sleigh behind a matched team of blacks on a clear night with stars above and white snow around, with me and grandpa nestled warm and cozy beneath a buffalo robe? My own children have never known this luxury at all. Today we read about these things or see them in the Currier and Ives prints.   *Dr. Harold C. Urey*

WORLD PEACE

In the swift flow of daily events it is easy to lose track of the broad strategy of our foreign policy. We seek peace, of course. But we seek it in what seems to us the only dependable way—the substitution of justice and law for force.

This is a relatively recent concept and even today many do not accept it.

Often peace is identified with the imposition by strong nations of their "benevolent" rule upon the weaker. Most of these efforts collapsed in war. The best known effort of this kind was the *Pax Romana*. And a *Pax Britannica* for a century kept relative peace and a world order which promoted world-wide economic development.

But the world of today is very different from the world of past centuries. It cannot be ruled.

Nevertheless, world peace through world rule is the creed of International Communism.

The reasoning is very simple. Physical matter, these Communists see, becomes more productive when it is ordered, when there are no disharmonies, when there is no grit in the gears. Human beings, they believe, are but animated particles of matter and should be treated in the same way as matter, if maximum productivity and harmony are to be achieved. So, it is argued, people everywhere should be brought into world order and conformity of action, thought and belief. This is the mission of the International Communist movement.

We and our allies reject this road to peace, no matter how trying and difficult may be the alternative. We know that human beings are more than animated particles of matter. They are part of a spiritual world.   *John Foster Dulles*

RUSSIA IN PERSPECTIVE

To understand and place in perspective what one sees in Russia some background of general knowledge regarding the country is helpful. Here is a nation extending 2,000 miles from North to South and 6,000 miles from West to East. It covers about one-sixth of the world's land surface, having approximately two and one-half times the area of the United States, including Alaska and Hawaii. This is the world's largest unbroken land mass under one flag. There are over 30,000 miles of coastline, but only one major unrestricted port—Murmansk—with access to the open sea throughout the year.

The Soviet population of 209 million compares to 175 million for the United States. Forty-three per cent of the people live in the cities in contrast to 64 per cent in the United States. Moscow with five million population, Leningrad with over three million and Kiev, Baku and a number of other cities each with around a million population are the largest cities. The people of this nation speak one hundred and forty-nine languages.

Forests cover an area about equal to the area of the United States and constitute a large portion of the entire world's timber reserves. The Soviet Union is also rich in oil, iron ore and manganese, and is perhaps the richest country in the world in minerals. If you combine important natural resources with hard work by the entire population, austerity in the consumption of consumer goods, and substantial saving with heavy investment in plant and equipment, you have the basic reasons why the authorities in the Kremlin believe they will inevitably attain economic and political leadership of the world. Some of the best informed observers of the Russian economy are convinced that the Kremlin authorities believe it is only a matter of time until they surpass us.   *Herbert V. Prochnow*

AMERICA'S MESSAGE

We have heard much of the phrase, "peace and friendship." This phrase, in expressing the aspiration of America, is not complete. We should say instead, "peace and friendship, in freedom." This, I think, is America's real message to the world.
Dwight D. Eisenhower

FAITH

Today we are the only nation in the world that expresses faith in God upon the coin of the realm. But we are not alone in our faith. Our national motto reflects the heartfelt conviction of all mankind.   *General Bruce C. Clarke*

CHRISTIANITY OR COMMUNISM

One of the great challenges of Communism is that is gives to men a complete philosophy of life, a philosophy that is logical —if you make the first assumption! That assumption is that this is a materialistic world and that the fundamental fact in the world is matter, working itself out in a dialectical method which inevitably will produce Communism. But if, on the other hand, Christianity is true, if the fundamental thing in the world is not matter but God and His will, then Christianity is realistic, for it is related to the very way in which the universe is constructed. *Anson Phelps Stokes, Jr.*

THE NATION LEFT BEHIND

The sad fact is that while we all dwell on the same globe and use the same calendar, hundreds of millions of people are living centuries back in terms of economic, social and political progress. For them, the world has stood still. In some countries oxen slowly thresh grain by treading it under foot just as they did two thousand years ago. The women of Jericho go to the well for water and carry it in earthen jugs on their heads just as they did in the days of Abraham, Isaac and Jacob. The nations that were left behind now provide Communism, with its promises of rapid industrial progress, a vast field of perhaps one billion five hundred million people in which to work.

Herbert V. Prochnow

HE TAKES HIS BURDENS ALONG

One asked Socrates why it was that Alcibiades, who was so brilliant and able a man, and had traveled so much, and seen so much of the world, was nevertheless so unhappy a man. Socrates replied, "Because wherever he goes Alcibiades takes himself with him." *Clarence Edward Macartney*

LOOKING OUT FOR YOURSELF

When some people say, "Well, I must look out for myself; if I don't look out for myself, nobody will," I wonder what self they are thinking of. Years ago, in one of his first books, Dr. Fosdick explained this in the following illustration: As children we used to have a box of blocks, and when we turned it over, a smaller block would come out. Then, if we turned it back again, a still smaller one would come out until there was a whole row of blocks, a big one at one end and a tiny little one at the other end. Now, when one says, "I must look out for myself," which self does he mean, asked Dr. Fosdick, the little one at the one end or the great big one at the other end? Washington might have saved his Virginia planter self and lost his larger self, the Father of his Country. Jesus might have saved his carpenter of Nazareth self and lost his larger self, the Saviour of the World.   *J. Walter Malone*

WHERE THE SUN SHINES

Red Oak, Iowa, is situated in a valley. The railroad station is upon a hill. Standing on the platform of the railroad station you can look down and see all the homes in one easy glance. On one occasion I was talking to a little girl who was standing there and, not knowing her well at all, I said: "Tell me which one of these houses you live in." The sun was shining brightly, flickering through the trees and on the houses, and she answered: "You mean the *house* that I live in? I live in a *home*."

"Yes," I said, "but what's the difference?" "Well," she replied, "the sun shines *on* a house, but it shines *in* a home."
                    Robert E. Edgar

TO BE OR NOT TO BE

Dr. Fosdick says one of the constant fears of human life is that of deciding. Hesitation and reluctance hold sway. We want someone else to decide for us, or at least help us to decide. This business of making decisions is the hub of the wheel of life. In a World Series baseball game think how little time some of these men have to make a decision. With the batter, how few seconds he has from the time the ball leaves the pitcher's hand until it crosses the plate to make his decision, to swing or let it go by. These are "split-second" decisions. Fortunately for us, the majority of ours are not made under that pressure. But like the batter, decide we must. The umpire decides for us if we fail to decide. So Life is a great Umpire. Every ball crossing the plate forces a decision upon you, and if you fail to make up your mind, then Time, the Old Umpire, calls them for you. This world has not been put together by Hamlets who hesitate with, "To be or not to be." And this world is not going to be saved by any such cowardly indecision.   *Clinton C. Cox*

HOW NATIONS GROW

In a free society, free men choose to save and invest for economic growth. In a regimented society, the state dictates the rate of saving and the character of the investment. In any society, investment must be for productive purposes if the standards of living of the people are to be improved. Building pyramids did not make a thriving, vigorous Egyptian economy. There is no easy route to economic growth. Saving means self-denial. It means not consuming now in order to produce more later. To achieve economic progress, every nation must save and invest. There are no short cuts through easy money and artificial low interest rates. There are no exceptions. These are economic imperatives. The nation that neglects them does so at the risk of its economic survival.   *'Herbert V. Prochnow*

AMERICAN FREEDOM ON TRIAL

Here is where our American freedom is on trial today. It is not on trial in Russia. It is not on trial among the satellite countries. It is on trial here. Can the individual men and women in our nation achieve that discipline of character and intelligence requisite to preserve, extend and enhance our freedom? If not, then American freedom is a broken reed for those who look to it for strength and support, and sooner or later it will be exchanged for the iron rod to totalitarianism or the steel cage of bureaucracy. We simply cannot keep and enjoy freedom without deserving it and bearing with its burdens. I think that beyond all question disillusionment with freedom because of its burdens and hazards is freedom's most seductive peril.

Dr. Robert Worth Frank

DENYING MAN'S HIGHEST IDEALS

To accept an endless succession of bloody, utterly indecisive wars as the will of God or as the last, best hope of men is to me the supreme blasphemy against both God and man. To say that because men always have fought bloody wars, so they always must and will fight them is to say that men prefer evil to good, force to reason, death to life, hate to love, agony to joy. It is to say that God has no concern with our world and that men have no power to think His thoughts after Him or to learn to do His will. It is to deny the validity of man's highest ideals, the rightness of his noblest purposes, and it is to say that his piled-up sacrifices have all been made in vain. It is to say that Christ was born and taught to little purpose and that there is no power on earth or in heaven, in God or in man able to make us come off victorious, not over each other, but over the loveless, Godless wilderness which we ourselves have made, the wilderness of greed, and fear and hate through which the Four Horsemen ride. *Boynton Merrill*

THE QUALITIES WE NEED

If Russia with its bleak and barren materialism becomes in history a blind Samson who pushes down the economic temple of the capitalist world, it will be because weaknesses had developed in the temple before the shoulders of communism were brought against its pillars. It will not be because of the spiritual and secular strength of communism. It will not be because communism has subordinated man and made him the serf of the state. It will be because you and I have failed. It will be because our ideals, our vision, our character and our minds were not equal to the challenge of democracy, freedom, and modern capitalism with its sense of social responsibility.

Herbert V. Prochnow

HE REFUSED TO HATE

The late Daniel C. Roper, former Secretary of Commerce, related an interesting experience to me some months before he died. Mr. Roper was a Southerner who loved the South and its great traditions. He said, "A Yankee from Vermont came to see me recently. What do you think he wanted me to do? He, a Yankee, actually wanted me to join with him in raising funds to erect a great memorial in honor of Robert E. Lee for the nation's capital." He continued, "I thought about it a good deal and wondered why. I know that all Americans love Robert E. Lee, this man who served his country so well and at last faced the tragic choice of remaining loyal to his state of Virginia or to the United States of America. He made his choice, and led the Confederate armies. He was a rebel, and yet he is loved by the North against whom he rebelled. Why?" Mr. Roper said, "I have read his writings carefully, and you cannot find the word 'enemy' in any letter or statement of Robert E. Lee. He refused to hate. That was a purpose. Neither war nor military necessity divorced him from that purpose." Said Mr. Roper, "I think that's why we Americans today, North and South, respect him."

G. Bromley Oxnam

FIRST THINGS FIRST

We are at a dangerous stage. Great material wealth, limitless powers and vast "know-how" are all ours. We still recall and we like to mouth the great words like faith, and liberty, and justice, and God and moral purpose. But John Foster Dulles said in his *War or Peace* that it was our fathers who really believed in these things and who were motivated by their august meanings. We, you and I, are apt to toss them around easily, as children do "eeny, meeny, miney, mo"; but much of the splendor has gone out of them because we really trust in atom bombs and in great assembly lines, in the marvels of mass production, and more and more we depend upon the compulsions of government rather than on the drive of the enlightened moral individual.

America will be truly great and her influence will sway the mind and the behavior of the world toward justice and brotherhood and peace only when she puts first things first. "We must," said Mr. Dulles, "reject totally the Marxian thesis that material things are primary and spiritual things only secondary . . . We must not be afraid to recapture faith in the primacy of human liberty and freedom, and to hold to the religious view that man is destined by God to be more than a material producer, and that his chief end is something more than physical security."

Boynton Merrill

THE WONDER OF MAN

In Marc Connolly's play, *Green Pastures,* the negro folk version of the Bible, "De Lawd," before the creation of man, when apparently celestial existence for him and the angels was more leisurely and less harried than it ever has been since then, is asked by Gabriel in an off-hand moment to pass a miracle. Gabriel, you may recall, liked wonders. "De Lawd" seems reluctant to comply. "When you pass one miracle," he says, "you got to rare back and pass another miracle. That's the trouble with miracles." Finally, "De Lawd" says he will pass one more miracle, the most important miracle of all. And after a deep breath he issues the command, "Let there be man." Since then, man has been a miracle to himself, in the sense of a wonder and a mystery, whenever he has paused long enough in the strenuous business of living to reflect upon his own nature and its potentialities.

Too often, however, man has taken himself casually and for granted, when he has not held a thoroughly disparaging view of himself. You may recall Emerson's saying that if the stars came out only once every century, what preparations we should make for the event, and with what breathless awe we should view the sublime spectacle. But because they appear each night we take them for granted and seldom notice them. It is often thus with these human selves, other selves and our own.

In the great creative literary and artistic epochs of history it has been otherwise, however. The giant minds have been profoundly impressed with the wonder of man. Sophocles, in the golden age of Pericles, hymns this wonder in the ode from the chorus of *Antigone.*

"Wonders are many, and none is more wonderful than man." He crosses the sea and yearly plows the earth; he can capture for his purpose bird, beast and fish. He hath taught himself speed and wind-swift thought, and the temper that rules in cities. He hath built "shelter from frost and the shafts of rain." "Yea, he hath resource for all . . ." "Only against Death shall he call for aid in vain." *Dr. Robert Worth Frank*

THE NEED FOR CRITICAL EXAMINATION

Private enterprise is today capable of producing goods on such a gigantic scale that it is dependent as never before upon the economic well-being of the masses of people. The tens of millions of Americans who constitute our markets must have the means and the willingness to buy the products of industry if the economy is to operate at the high level of activity which is the accepted objective of business, labor and government. At this point, the economic concerns of private business, labor and government are identical.

Mass production by modern, power-driven industry is now capable of producing an endless flow of goods. Mass markets, therefore, become imperative. We have moved steadily away from the sedative hum of the hand spinning wheel and the village feed mill to huge gray factories. Great power-driven factories, great organizations of labor and great markets make highly improbable any broad return of government to the Arcadian simplicity of Colonial days.

As President Eisenhower stated, "The demands of modern life and the unsettled status of the world require a more important role for government than it played in earlier and quieter times."

But this does not mean that we should now thoughtlessly turn over the management of the economy to an all-powerful state. It means that we need more than ever critically to examine the role of government.   *Herbert V. Prochnow*

SIX CRISES

The minds of thoughtful Americans today are greatly troubled. It ill-befits these times, or you and me, that I should try to entertain you with the usual after-lunch quips and humor. It is more fitting that I speak bluntly of our difficulties, and try to give you some assurance of the fundamental strengths of America.

We are in the midst of 6 dangerous crises.

We have in the Communist nations implacable enemies, whose determination—despite their disguises of peaceful cooperation—is to destroy and dominate the free world. And they are succeeding at our very doorstep.

We are not only plagued with their conspiracies but with the infection of Karl Marx in both the thinking of our people and the actions of our own governments.

We are in a crisis of inflation, which steadily saps the earnings and savings of our people.

We are in a crisis in our foreign trade—in which competition and an unfavorable trade balance cause the flight of our capital from fear of the stability of the dollar.

We are in a crisis of the domination of some labor unions by hoodlums; and the use of their gigantic funds to influence elections.

We are in the midst of an increasing moral slump as witness the increase in major known crimes.   *Herbert Hoover*

THE GROWTH OF NATIONAL STRENGTH

I have lived a long life, and I have seen our nation rally, exert its strengths to surmount dangers as great as those which beset us today.

Among the signs of our moral and spiritual strength, I have witnessed the outpouring of compassion which saved the world from two gigantic famines that followed the two great wars. During forty-five years we provided the necessary margins of food, medical care and clothing to 1,400,000,000 human beings —who would otherwise have perished. And included among them were millions of people in our implacable enemy—Communist Russia.

And in these efforts we have restored healthy minds and bodies to over 16,000,000 children—who would have died from famine and disease—or would have become a danger to the world with their degenerate minds and dwarfed bodies.

Within my span of years, I have seen our voluntary organizations and institutions—devoted to religious service, charity, education, and community welfare—increase by tens of thousands in numbers and by billions of dollars in support.

I have witnessed elementary education expand to include practically all our children. Whatever complaints may be made about the system, it has practically abolished illiteracy; and it has embedded in children's minds the inspiring names and events of our history.

I have witnessed the growth of higher education until today our institutions of learning are turning out more instructed men and women each year than the rest of the world combined.

I have witnessed great discoveries from scientific research. With the advance of medical science, our youth are taller than their fathers, and the span of life has been greatly extended.

We can well respect the accomplishments of Russian technicians. But let us not forget that they obtained the telegraph, the telephone, the electric lamp, the speaking sound track, the radio broadcast tube, the airplane, atomic and nuclear power from us.   *Herbert Hoover*

WE NEED ALL OUR STRENGTHS

If we take a worm's eye view of the crises and forces which surround us, we may worry that we are approaching the decline and fall of the greatest nation in history.

If we take a bird's eye view, we see the fundamental strength of the American people.

And how can this strength be sustained and expanded?

It must come from growth of religious faith; from our devotion to freedom of men; and from a determined staunch stand against the evils which beset us. With these forces in motion, there can be no decline or fall in this nation.

But we have need to exert all the strengths which God has given our Nation.   *Herbert Hoover*

TWO GREAT QUESTIONS CONFRONT US

First, in the years immediately ahead will we limit the role of government to those functions which private individuals cannot perform as well—or will we as a people gradually become less self-reliant, less willing to assume responsibilities and seek increasingly the delusive shelter and deceptive security of government?

The second question confronts all of mankind, and the answer to it may well determine the survival of the Free World. Will the masses over the world forsake their freedom, destroy the ideals which make the good society, and give up even their religious faith for materialism in their fierce determination to achieve social and economic progress rapidly—or will it be possible within the framework of freedom to achieve social and economic progress for the restless masses, to enrich and exalt man in contrast to the state, and to hold securely to those priceless values in a free society that lie far beyond goods and guns?   *Herbert V. Prochnow*

THE ROLE OF GOVERNMENT

Millions of Americans condemn the expanding role of government. They protest increasing government expenditures, unbalanced budgets and high taxes. At the same time through their representatives in the Congress they demand of government vast new services, Federal aid, price supports, stockpiling of products on a gigantic scale, bonuses and subsidies. Approximately 100 Federal programs provide aid for states. We persist in indulging in the pleasant illusion that Federal aid does not come from local taxpayers. The increasing role of government over the years offers little encouragement to those who believe that government should perform essentially only those functions which individuals, businesses and communities cannot perform, or cannot perform as well as government. If this trend is to be halted, we shall need a major change in our thinking. This is not now evident. We shall need far greater self-reliance, or we shall inevitably lose more and more of the private economy of the United States and find ourselves finally embracing the economic socialization which now characterizes the communist world.   *Herbert V. Prochnow*

CARRYING HEAVY BURDENS

A few months ago I read a poignant and beautiful story written by one whom some of you here surely have known, Dorothy Canfield Fisher. It is the simple, searching story of a physically powerful but dull-witted farm hand who spent all his life in a little Vermont village and valley. His whole life was made difficult and sad by the bitter tongue of his mother who resented him from the day he was born. He had a rather foolish grin. "Shut your mouth, Lem, you look like a born fool": that from the one who from his cradle should have loved him, but who, from his cradle, was cantankerous and full of scoldings. Yet, with dogged faithfulness he served her till she died. He was, from childhood up, the target of the jibes of the children (and how cruel children can be!). He was the butt of jokes in the village store; until, upon a hillside pasture one black night he came on a huge dog killing sheep. He had no weapon and, alone, in the dark he strangled the dog to death with his bare hands and then, in the morning, when the men went out to bury the sheep and see whose dog it really was they found he had killed a great timber wolf strayed down from Canada. From that day forward there was cautious awe of him, tacit admiration.

All his life long (it is the theme of the story) Lem carried heavy burdens; his mean mother, also an unwed girl in the village and her baby. Innocent of wrong as the village brook, he took the shame that the baby might have a name. The mother died in a year and Lem "raised" the little girl. Later she married and her baby soon was desperately ill. Lem sold all his sheep to get money to save the baby's life and that done, penniless and worn out, he died, refusing medicine, saying only, "I'm real tired." No one else would touch these and other burdens like them. Someone had to. Lem did, in his fumbling way. It is a beautiful story of a very brave, of a very good man and, of a man lonely almost beyond belief.

Yes, lonely people can of themselves do something about their loneliness. They can lose it, as Lem did, by caring for others who are far needier than they.   *Boynton Merrill*

MEANINGLESS TALK

How much valuable time is wasted in meaningless chit-chat! When the telephone was invented, someone told Thoreau that now the people in Massachusetts could talk to the people in Texas. Thoreau wisely questioned, "But suppose the people in Massachusetts have nothing to say to the people in Texas?"
Sidney W. Powell

THE PREY OF FEAR

Men are as apt as women to allow their imaginations to run rampant. A man retired and hardly knew what to do with himself. As a result he became the prey of morbid fear. Explaining how he spent his time, he said, "I get up early, read the obituary column, and if my name isn't there, I go back to bed!"

Kenneth Hildebrand

THE RECORD OF AMERICAN CAPITALISM

Soviet Russia is not now, if it ever was, a classless society. Contrary to the philosophy of Karl Marx and Friedrich Engels, Communism is increasingly adopting rewards and incentives in industry and in education. There are sharp class distinctions, particularly in wage and fringe benefits. It is largely the higher paid classes in the Soviet economy who can buy the relatively small volume of consumer durable goods available. They are able to have automobiles, better housing, better clothing and perhaps even servants. In the United States, in contrast to the Soviet Union, masses of people receive relatively high incomes, and consumer goods are produced in quantity so that tens of millions of Americans can buy automobiles, washing machines, refrigerators and other durable goods. It is the United States, the leading capitalist nation of the world, which has given the masses of people the highest standard of living in history.

Herbert V. Prochnow

AN EXPERIENCE IN SOVIET RUSSIA

I had an unforgettable experience in one of several churches I visited behind the Iron Curtain. Three services are held in this church in Moscow each Sunday as well as a number during the week. On my visit I was seated at the railing in the balcony. The church was filled from top to bottom with the aisles crowded by those standing. For example, a mother entered with children and had to stand with the children at the end of a pew. Occasionally, someone who was seated arose to permit a person who was standing to be seated. Some in the aisles were on their knees. They may have found it difficult to stand through the entire service which lasted two hours with two sermons. The text for the first sermon was "Trust in the Living God," and it was from Timothy I, Chapter IV, Verse 10. Here and there throughout the congregation there was weeping. I saw very poorly dressed people generously contribute to the collection, and I was told that finances are not a problem of the church. As I looked into the many hundreds of earnest, deeply sincere faces in that congregation and saw the care-lined, gentle features of the older women with their babushkas, I felt certain that no government, no matter how determined and powerful, could completely destroy the living faith, the cherished ideals, and the eternal values of the common people of Russia.   *Herbert V. Prochnow*

COMPETITION WITH SOVIET RUSSIA

When Mr. Khrushchev says the competition is between communism and capitalism, he misses the point on two counts.

Even on economic grounds, it would be more accurate to call it a competition between two forms of capitalism—one state controlled, the other controlled by the independent, free market decisions and choices of literally millions of individuals. And even on these same narrow economic grounds, we are convinced that free capitalism—creative individualism—can outproduce any form of state capitalism, just as it has up to now.

But the march of civilization cannot and must not be confined merely to economic systems. That is why Mr. Khrushchev's so-called historical analysis in which he traces a line of progress from feudalism to capitalism to communism falls down. History cannot be judged solely in material and economic terms. When we analyze these three systems in terms of freedom for the individual, we find that the change from feudalism to private capitalism was one from less freedom to more freedom. And a change now to communism would be going back rather than forward—exactly the reverse of progress. . . .

We are proud of the fact that 31 million Americans own their own homes. But what is even more important is that in this country a man's home is truly his castle. He has absolute protection against unreasonable search and seizure or confiscation of his property by the state.

It is indeed noteworthy to point out that 56 million Americans own their own automobiles. But what is even more important is that they can drive these automobiles anywhere they wish without travel permits and internal passports.

The fact that Americans own 50 million television sets and 143 million radio sets is a tribute to our industrial progress. But far more important is that those who speak over the airways can say what they wish without government censorship, and those who own the sets have true freedom of choice as to what they hear and see.

Our homes, our highways, our motor cars and electronic marvels are not ends in themselves but only the means, the necessary foundations for a life of cultural and spiritual richness. For us this must be a life of individual freedom and human dignity, a life that liberates the human spirit of every restraint beyond its own inherent capability and then goes on to expand and increase that capability.

In this peaceful competition, therefore, let us test our systems to see which provides for individual human beings the greater opportunities for personal freedom and personal expression.

Richard M. Nixon

CHAPTER VII

WORTHWHILE THOUGHTS

ISN'T IT THE TRUTH?

I'm careful of the words I say, to keep them soft and sweet.
I never know from day to day which ones I'll have to eat!

A CHINESE PROVERB

If there is righteousness in the heart, there will be beauty
in the character. If there is beauty in the character, there will
be love in the home. If there is love in the home, there will be
order in the nation. If there is order in the nation, there will
be peace in the world.

MINDS

Great minds discuss ideas; average minds discuss events; very
small minds discuss people.

THE REWARD

The reward life holds for work well done is increased capacity, greater difficulties, and more work.

TOO BUSY

If you're too busy to pray, you're *too* busy.

DEATH

Everyone ought to fear to die until he has done something
that will always live.

STILL BIGGER

A big man is not one who makes no mistakes, but one who
is bigger than any mistakes he makes.   *American Eagle*

SUCCESS

One of the most important aspects of the pecuniary measure
of success is seen in the "externalization" of our lives. We are

more anxious to *seem* than to *be*. We strive for baubles and gee-gaws and gimcracks, good clothes and shiny cars, rather than for contentment, fundamental culture and appreciation of real beauty. Not knowing how to spend our time, we take what satisfaction we can in spending our money.   *John Ise*

INDUSTRY

After a great deal of experience and observation, I have become convinced that industry is a better horse to ride than genius. It may never carry any man as far as genius has carried individuals, but industry—patient, steady, intelligent industry —will carry thousands into comfort, and even celebrity; and this it does with absolute certainty.   *Walter Lippmann*

YOU CAN'T CUT DOWN THE CLOUDS!

When Henry David Thoreau, the nature-lover, saw the woodsman's axe destroying the forest, he exclaimed: "Thank God, they cannot cut down the clouds!"

There are some eternal things that the destructive powers of men cannot destroy. To think on these things is to achieve an inward quiet and peace, even in a world torn with misunderstandings and prejudices.

DISCONTENT

There are two kinds of discontent in this world: the discontent that works, and the discontent that wrings its hands. The first gets what it wants, and the second loses what it had. There is no cure for the first but success, and there is no cure at all for the second.   *Elbert Hubbard*

FREE ENTERPRISE

We shall not be able to preserve our form of enterprise over the next 50 years simply by praising it.   *Donald K. Dean*

THE DANGER

When the goal of a country is only pleasure and comfort, there is danger.   *Carl Sandburg*

FOR OTHERS

What we have done for ourselves alone, dies with us; what we have done for others and the world, remains and is immortal.
Albert Pike

VALUES

Spires outlast spears; altars are more lasting than armament; freedom, truth, love are invincible. They belong to the stuff of eternity.   *Dr. Joseph R. Sizoo*

AGE

Age is not so much a matter of gray hair as it is of gray matter. Beauty is more the result of how you make up your mind than how you make up your face.
Rev. Robert C. Howe, Christian Advocate

A WINDOW

The Bible is a window of hope thru which we look into eternity.   *Missionary Tidings*

WHAT GOES ON INSIDE

It does not matter too much what the outside of a boy or girl looks like—any more than it matters what the outside of a house looks like. It is what goes on inside that counts. The grandest mansion in the country can be a very unhappy home, while the simplest cottage can be the happiest place in the world.

REST

A wise old woman said, "I've so much to do I don't know where to start, so I think I'll sit down first and have a rest, and then that'll be done, at any rate."   *Margaret Ryan*

WEALTH AND POVERTY

The difference between a poor man and a millionaire is that one worries over his next meal and the other over his last.

GENIUS

A genius is a man who shoots at something no one else can see, and hits it.

KEEP WORKING

It's all right with the Lord if you pray for a good harvest— but He expects you to keep right on plowing.

William Feather

A BETTER JOB

Most of us could find a better job, and usually it will be the one we're doing now.

YOUTH

Youth must learn to listen before it speaks, as the wheat must absorb before it can produce the grain.

Bishop Fulton J. Sheen

IF YOU DESPAIR

Never despair; but if you do, work on in despair.

Edmund Burke

POLITICS

Politics when divorced from education and religion becomes a poor and petty thing. *Glen Frank*

PURPOSE OF LIFE

Strange is our situation here upon earth. Each comes for a short visit, not knowing why, yet seeming to divine a purpose. There is one thing we do know: Man is here for the sake of other men—above all, for those upon whose well-being our own happiness depends, . . . and for the countless unknown souls with whose fate we are connected by a bond of sympathy.

Albert Einstein

AFTER THE EVENT

Those who are only wise after the event should hold their peace. *Winston Churchill*

FAITH

No ray of sunlight is ever lost, but the green which it awakes into existence needs time to sprout, and it is not always granted to the sower to see the harvest. All work that is worth anything is done in faith.   *Albert Schweitzer*

THE PURPOSE OF EDUCATION

The true purpose of education is to cherish and unfold the seed of immortality already sown within us; to develop, to their fullest extent, the capacities of every kind with which the God who made us has endowed us.

Anna Jameson, Education Digest

CHRISTIANITY

Mussolini is dead—Hitler is dead—Stalin is dead. And when Communism dies the church will still be here to preach its funeral.   ***Rev. B. B. Pennington, Christian Advocate***

THE WORK OF THE AUTHOR

I have the feeling that more and more books are being sold about escaping from prison with a toothpick, or walking up the Amazon on stilts. This is all very well, but the greatest prison to escape from is the prison of the ego, and the most dangerous journey is the journey of our day-to-day living. If one can describe these things with force, with passion, with style, with wit, one will create literature.   *J. B. Priestley, British author*

THE NON-CONFORMISTS

Those who have done most for the world and lifted the level of life in their generation have been the dissenters and non-conformists. They have been of resolute purpose and staunch principle. They have had standards and kept them, no matter what the cost.   *Robert J. McCracken*

THE MOTIVE POWER

At the summit of every noble human endeavor, you will find a steeple pointing toward God.

Dr. Mack Stokes, Emory University

OUR PROBLEM

Prosperity? We Americans are the few people in the world who have to ask "How can I reduce?" and "Where can I park?" *Burton Hillis, Better Homes & Gardens*

THE REAL TRAGEDY

The tragedy of life is not that people die, it is that they never truly live. *Dr. Leonard A. Stidley, Christian Advocate*

NOT CERTAIN

The hydrogen bomb is here to stay, but I sometimes wonder whether the human race is. *W. Sterling Cole*

DEBT

A new Beatitude might well read, Blessed are the young, for they shall inherit the national debt. *Herbert Hoover*

THE MEANING OF LIFE

The young person seeks an answer to the question, *What shall I do with my life?* What such a person wants—what we all want—is a meaning that becomes a motivating force in our lives. And when we ask this question, whether we are conscious of it or not, we have begun to think religiously.
Nathan M. Pusey

THE GREAT EXPERIENCE

The most beautiful thing we can experience is the mysterious. It is the source of all true art and science. He to whom this emotion is a stranger, who can no longer pause to wonder and stand rapt in awe, is as good as dead: his eyes are closed.
Albert Einstein

INTELLECTUAL UNIFORMITY

Democracy cannot survive where there is such uniformity that everyone wears exactly the same intellectual uniform or point of view. *Bishop Fulton J. Sheen*

THE VALUE OF TIME

Time is one of God's greatest gifts, and yet how often men devise ingenious methods to make it pass lightly and quickly, and refer to it as "killing time."

The value of time arises from:

1. Its brevity. The time is short. "The longest life is short."
2. Its uncertainty. "Boast not thyself of tomorrow."
3. The fact that it is irrecoverable. The hand on the clock can never be turned back.

Time is given that we may prepare for eternity. The watchword of the moment should be "now."

THE LITTLE THINGS

They tell a story of the mighty oak which stood on the skyline of the Rockies. It survived the hail, the heavy snows, the storms, the bitter cold of many years. Then it finally was felled by an attack of little beetles. And so it is with marriage. It is the little hurt, the little neglect, the little things a couple forget to do for each other that blights their relationship.

Roy A. Burkhart

THE TRUTH

Slowly the truth is being recognized that a higher standard of living can be achieved in this country only thru more production per man, whether on the farm, in the factory, or in any productive capacity.   *J. K. Stern, Hoard's Dairyman*

BROTHERS

The answer to the question, "Am I my brother's keeper?" must always be "No—! I am my brother's brother."

Paul Klapper

THE SHEEP AND THE WOLVES

The church is suffering more from the sheepishness of the sheep than from the wolfishness of the wolves.

Present Truth Messenger

THE LAW OF LOVE

Everything in creation obeys the law of love. There is no tree that bears fruit for its own use; the sun does not shine for itself. It is only man and the devil who in everything seek their own. *Anders Nygren, Agape and Eros (Westminster)*

WISDOM

A little girl, taken to church regularly by her parents, was asked what a saint was. Knowing about them principally from the stained-glass windows of her church, the child replied: "A saint is somebody that the light shines thru."

Industrial Press Service

MISTAKES

It takes courage and character to defend the right of others to say what we believe to be mistaken. But respect for knowledge prompts us to believe that mistakes have a way of refuting themselves.

E. B. Fred, Former President, University of Wisconsin

ARE WE FOREIGNERS?

I thought that foreign children
Lived far across the sea,
Until I got a letter
From a boy in Italy.
"Dear little foreign friend," it said
As plainly as could be.
Now I wonder who is "foreign"—
The other child or me?
Ethel Blair Jordan, Phi Delta Kappan

DEEDS COUNT

The smallest good deed is better than the grandest good intention. *Duguet*

GOOD ADVICE

If you know it all, bow low. *Chinese Proverb*

THE NEW LEAF

He came to my desk with quivering lip. The lesson was done. "Have you a new leaf for me, dear Teacher? I have spoiled this one!"

I took his leaf, all soiled and blotted, and gave him a new one, all unspotted. Then, into his tired heart I smiled, "Do better now, my Child!"

I went to the throne, with trembling heart. The year was done. "Have you a new year for me, dear Master? I have spoiled this one!"

He took my year, all soiled and blotted, and gave me a new one, all unspotted. Then into my tired heart he smiled, "Do better now, my Child!"   *Kathleen Wheeler*

SUCCESS

This is success: To be able to carry money without spending it; to be able to bear an injustice without retaliating; to be able to keep on the job until it is finished; to be able to do one's duty even when one is not watched; to be able to accept criticism without letting it whip you. *Selection from The Uplift, a monthly publication of the Stonewall Jackson Manual Training School of Concord, N. C.*

YESTERDAY AND TODAY

Dr. Margaret Mead, distinguished anthropologist and author, made a very interesting observation in an address not long ago. She pointed out that for a long time it was the universal custom to say on parting: "Good-bye," which is a shortened form of "God be with you." Today it is quite common instead to say: "Take it easy." *Halford & Robert Luccock, Pulpit Digest*

WHAT PRAYER DOES

When we flip a light switch we are completing the circuit which causes the bulb to light. When we turn off the light we are breaking the circuit and the light goes off. . . . Prayer completes the circuit between God and man. Without prayer this circuit is broken and the individual's life is without light. *Church & Home*

DOUBTFUL

"It probably would be all right if we'd love our neighbors as ourselves," a man on the bus remarked this morning, "but I wonder if they could stand that much affection."

Burton Hillis, Better Homes & Gardens

WORTH CONSIDERING

Vision is the art of seeing things that are invisible.

Dean Swift

To be content, just think how happy you would be if you lost everything you have right now, and then got it back again!

It is the highest form of self-respect to admit mistakes and to make amends for them.

Worry pulls tomorrow's cloud over today's sunshine.

Never quit because you have reached your goal. Nothing recedes like success.

The man who trusts men will make fewer mistakes than the man who distrusts men.

A good resolve—to do someone a good turn, and not be found out.

Many persons might have attained to wisdom had they not assumed they already possessed it.

AFFLICTION

Affliction comes to all not to make us sad, but sober; not to make us sorry, but wise; not to make us despondent, but its darkness to refresh us, as the night refreshes the day; not to impoverish, but to enrich us, as the plow enriches the field; to multiply our joy, as the seed, by planting, is multiplied a thousandfold.   *Henry Ward Beecher*

INANIMATE GUEST

When television sets first began to take over living rooms thruout the nation many parents understandably were bewildered and overwhelmed. If a loud-mouthed guest had settled himself in a corner and begun to tell raucous and unsuitable stories to the children, it seems likely that parents would have managed in some way to change the subject or get the children out of the room. Yet when an inanimate object began to do the same thing, consternation reigned in the household.   *Dorothy Barclay, New York Times*

THE DECLARATION OF INDEPENDENCE

On July 4, 1776, 56 serious-minded and dedicated men signed their names to a simple, impassioned document which they had named the Declaration of Independence. They were fully aware of the fact that this document would either bring freedom to all Americans, or else it would leave all 56 of them hanging from a gallows, to prove that their dream of national sovereignty had been folly. Only time would tell.

MOTHER

The future destiny of a child is always the work of a mother.
                              Napoleon Bonaparte
The mother's heart is the child's schoolroom.
                              Henry Ward Beecher
Men are what their mothers made them.
                              Ralph Waldo Emerson
Mother is the name for God in the lips and hearts of little children.   *Wm. Makepeace Thackeray*
God could not be everywhere, and so he made mothers.
                              Jewish Proverb
Women become like their mothers. That is their tragedy. No man does—that is his tragedy.   *Oscar Wilde*

> Years to a mother bring distress,
> But do not make her love the less.
>   *William Wordsworth*

SYMPATHY

Sympathy is two hearts tugging at one load.
                         Charles Henry Parkhurst

LISTEN

The other day I overheard a man maintain an unbroken monologue for half an hour. In vain his companion tried to cut in with a word now and then, but the steady flow of words continued uninterrupted. I could only think of the little quatrain that I learned as a boy:

> I love its gentle gurgle,
>   I love its fluent flow;
> I love to wind my mouth up,
>   And I love to hear it go.

All of us know how irritating it is to be the victim of this kind of monologue, especially when we ourselves have something to say.

I wonder if that is the way God sometimes feels about our prayers. There are some things *He* would like to say to *us,* but we give Him no chance. We turn the words of the boy Samuel around. With us it's not, "Speak, Lord, for Thy servant hears," but, "Listen, Lord, for Thy servant speaks."

I thought of this the other day as I passed a church whose front-lawn sign bore the words: *Don't talk so much when you pray; try listening.* Certainly prayer was never meant to be a one-way street. It was designed to carry traffic in both directions. If we have any place in the Heavenly Father's plan and purpose, there is undoubtedly guidance, warning, and encouragement which He wants to communicate to us.

The Reverend Richard W. Graves

REMOVING MOUNTAINS

The man who removes mountains begins by carrying away small stones.   *Chinese Proverb*

FREEDOM OF SPEECH

A Communist who uses freedom of speech to destroy freedom of speech has used the vehicle of words for an evil purpose, and is to be judged in exactly the same way as a motorist who uses his car to run down pedestrians.   *Bishop Fulton J. Sheen*

WORK

Nothing is really work unless one would rather do something else.

WORTH MEDITATION

It is not a question of who is right, but *what* is right.

Hardening of the heart ages people more quickly than hardening of the arteries.

Many a man can credit his success to the fact that he didn't have the advantages others had.

LIFE

Take Life just as though it was—and it is—an earnest, vital, and important affair. Take it as though you were born to the task of performing a merry part of it—as though the world awaited your coming. Take it as though it was a grand opportunity to do and achieve, to carry forward great and good schemes, to help and cheer a suffering, weary, or heartbroken brother.

Now and then a man stands aside from the crowd, labors earnestly, steadfastly, and confidently, and straightway becomes famous for wisdom, intellect, skill, greatness of some sort. The world wonders, admires, idolizes; and it only illustrates what others may do if they take hold of life with a purpose.

The miracle or the power that elevates the few is to be found in their industry, application, and perseverance, under the promptings of a brave, determined spirit.

Mark Twain (Samuel Langhorne Clemens)
humorist, lecturer, and author (1835-1910)

REAL HAPPINESS

I don't know what your destiny will be, but one thing I know: The only ones among you who will be really happy are those who have sought and found how to serve.

Albert Schweitzer

YOU MAY STUB YOUR TOE

You will never stub your toe standing still. The faster you go the more chance there is of stubbing your toe, but the more chance you have of getting somewhere.

Charles F. Kettering

THE CONTEST FOR AGES

The contest for ages had been to rescue liberty from the grasp of executive power.   *Daniel Webster*

GOOD DEEDS

Remember that if the opportunity for *great* deeds should never come, the opportunity for *good* deeds is renewed day by day. Let our ambition be goodness, not glory.   *Faber*

THE REAL PEACE PROGRAM

The real peace program has ten points, and those ten points are the Ten Commandments.   *Cardinal Francis J. Spellman*

WE NEED EACH OTHER

We need each other, as you will observe: "Very few men are wise by their own counsel, or learned by their own teaching; for he that was only taught by himself had a fool for his master.
Ben Jonson

CHOICE BITS

One kind of trouble is enough. Some folks take on three kinds at once—all they have now, all they have had, and all they ever expect to have.

There is nothing noble in being superior to some other person. True nobility lies in being superior to your previous self.

That which is given us by circumstance, fortune, accident, or chance, can be taken away by the same means. That which we have *become,* is eternal.   *Sunshine Magazine*

THE SECRET

The secret of education is never to forget the possibility of greatness.   *Gilbert Highet, Man's Unconquerable Mind*

DEEDS—NOT WORDS

Brotherhood is as nothing when it is expressed exclusively in words; it is as everything when it is expressed in deeds.
Missions

CHAPTER VIII

INTERESTING FACTS AND INTERESTING IDEAS

THEY'LL LEARN

The younger generation will learn the value of money when it begins paying off our debts.

TWO VIEWS

You can have the guy who's always searching for the bright side; I'll take the one who's in there polishing up the dull.

Don Marshall, Partners

IN THE PAST

In 1900, all of the hard-surfaced roads in the U. S. would not have linked New York and Boston. *Automobile Facts*

GOOD QUESTION

If women's intuition is so good, how come they have to ask so many questions? *Pipe Dreams*

THE SPACE AGE

Says Walter Sullivan, chief science writer for the New York Times: "School children 1,000 years from now will learn that the Space Age began in 1957-58. More than we possibly realize, these years mark the beginning of mankind's steps into space. Man in his quest for space knowledge can be compared to a potato bug in a sack of potatoes in the hold of a great ship, wondering what makes the ship go. Knowledge of space and the universe is minute compared to what remains to be learned."

INDEPENDENT THOUGHT

To destroy the Western tradition of independent thought it is not necessary to burn the books. All we have to do is to leave them unread for a couple of generations.

Robert M. Hutchins

OUR ASSOCIATES

One traveler moralizes that there is a law which tells us we tend to become like those with whom we habitually associate or admire. To live with Socrates must have resulted in becoming a wise man; to live with St. John, a loving and gentle person; to live with Paul, an earnest man; to live with Darwin and Audubon, a lover of nature. This truth may be expressed most forcefully in the words of another: "We become like those who are crowned in our hearts."

MOTHER'S WAY

He criticised her pudding, he didn't like her cake; he wished she'd make the biscuits his mother used to make. She didn't wash the dishes, and she didn't make a stew; and she didn't darn his stockings like his mother used to do.

So when one day he went the same old rigmarole through, she turned and boxed his ears, just like his mother used to do.

Speakers Library

TOO THICK

If someone asks you to fold a sheet of paper in half thirty times—look out! If you fold it once it becomes twice as thick; at the second fold it is four times as thick, at the third eight times. By the time you reach the seventh fold it is 128 times as thick; and if you could fold it thirty times, it would be over ten billion times as thick.

NO SUCH THING

A man drove his new Rolls-Royce over the Alps. Making a tight curve, his composure was jolted as the Rolls' front spring broke and left him to limp into the nearest Swiss town. He explained his problem by phone to Rolls-Royce, Ltd., in England. In no time, a representative arrived and replaced the spring.

Later, reviewing his bills, he noticed none from Rolls and asked them to check their records.

The manager of Rolls said, "There must be a mistake. There is no such thing as a broken spring on a Rolls-Royce!"

POWER

Experience hath shown that even under the best forms (of government), those entrusted with power have in time by slow operations perverted it into tyranny.   *Thomas Jefferson*

OUR MACHINE ECONOMY

In 1830, Peter Cooper's little steam locomotive, the *Tom Thumb,* proudly traveled thirteen miles at an average speed of six miles an hour. At that time, there were only twenty-three miles of railroad. By 1860, there were 30,000 miles and by 1890 over 160,000 miles. No other nation ever matched that expansion.

By 1860, the American factory system was firmly established. We had 140,000 manufacturing plants, and we were producing more goods by machine than by hand. This was a major turning point. The foundations of a machine economy had been firmly laid.   *Herbert V. Prochnow*

BRIBERY IN THE PAST

The Great Wall of China was decades in building, and was finished at the expense of vast treasure and thousands of human lives. It was intended for a defense against the marauding hordes of the north, who had so often laid waste to the land. However, historians tell us that within a short time of its completion it was pierced and proved inadequate, not because it was not massive and well enough built, but because of the human element—in each case the enemy bribed the guards.

SPEAKERS, TAKE NOTE

There is many a man who, when he has invented a phrase, thinks he has solved a problem.
     Sir Herbert Williams, British Parliament

LIFE IS LIKE THAT

Some of our novelists don't seem to care a hang what they do with their character's eyes. For instance:
     "Her eyes roamed carelessly around the room."
     "With her eyes she riveted him to the spot."

"He tore his eyes from her face and they fell on the letter at her feet."

"Their eyes met for a long, breathless moment, and swam together."

"Marjory would often take her eyes from the deck and cast them far out to sea."

"He wrenched his eyes away from hers. It was a painful moment for both of them."   *The Lookout*

HARD WORKERS

When you eat a spoonful of honey you probably have very little idea as to the amount of work and travel necessary to produce it. To make a pound of clover honey, bees must take the nectar from sixty-two thousand clover blossoms, and to do this requires two million, seven hundred and fifty thousand visits to the blossoms by the bees.

In other words, in order to collect enough nectar to make one pound of honey, a bee must go from hive to flower and back again two million, seven hundred and fifty thousand times. Then, when you think how far these bees sometimes have to fly in search of these clover fields—you get some idea of how hard they work.

ANTIQUES

Only uncomfortable chairs become antiques. The comfortable ones are worn out by use in a single generation.
                    Kiel (Wisconsin) Record

LOVELY AS A TREE

I think that I shall never see a billboard lovely as a tree. Perhaps, unless the billboards fall, I'll never see a tree at all!

THIS IS WORSE

It's bad to act like a fool, but it's worse when you're not acting.   *Atlas News*

WOMAN'S WORK

The woman's work that's never done is most likely what she asked her husband to do.

CIRCUMSTANTIAL EVIDENCE

If you would avoid suspicion, do not lace your shoes in a melon field.   *Chinese Proverb*

TV

Cowboys, Indians, wrestlers, and crime—what an awful waste of time! TV can amuse and educate, if we learn to discriminate!

FRIENDS

During the quail season, an old man was hunting with an ancient pointer. Twice the dog pointed. Each time the hunter walked over, kicked at the matted growth, wheeled sharply and fired into empty air.

Asked why, the old man explained: "I knew there warn't no birds in the grass. Old Jim's nose ain't what it used to be. But him and me have seen some wonderful days together. He's still trying hard and it'd be mighty little of me to call him a liar."   *Arkansas Baptist*

A NEW DRUG

Dr. Charles U. Leturneau of Chicago, praised a medicinal ingredient called "TLC" as a valuable discovery in treatment of the ailing.

"A new drug?" someone asked.

"No," replied the doctor. "Just 'tender, loving care.'"

SOME LABOR TOO

Learn to labor and to wait; but be careful how you start, lest you learn to wait so well, you overlook the labor part!   *Anonymous*

GOOD MANAGEMENT

A successful manager was asked what helped him reach the top. "One thing stands out," he said. "I could think out loud with my superiors. I could throw out crazy suggestions. I could talk over any subject without fear that I would be squelched. It had more effect upon my development as a manager than anything else."   *Harvard Business Review*

THE ULTIMATE GOAL

With strained nerves, tired bodies and cheated minds, we are paying the price of breathless living. Work faster. Play faster. Now, read faster. Where will it end? Will the next urge be for us to love faster, and sleep faster? Perhaps the ultimate goal is to die faster.   *Dwight Everett Watkins*

THE TEST OF A GOOD HOST

The test of being a good host is how well the departing guest likes himself.   *Marcelene Cox*

DOESN'T EVERYONE?

All I am or ever will be, I owe.
Mary Louise Wright, DeWitt (Arkansas) Era-Enterprise

GARDENING WE LIKE

The lazy way to enjoy a beautiful, productive garden is to live next door to one, and cultivate your neighbor.
Mrs. Richard Fisher, West Branch (Iowa) Times

NOTHING IS SAFE

Buses turn over,
Airplanes crash;
Trains are wrecked
And autos smash.
Hikers are slaughtered,
Ships can sink.
Better stay home
Is what I think.   *Phoenix Flame*

A GOOD SPEECH

A speech that's full of sparkling wit will keep its hearers grinning, provided that the end of it is close to the beginning!
Sunshine Magazine

THIS MAKES IT EASIER?

Habits don't have a hold on you—you have a hold on them.
Wildrooter

FEROCIOUS DRIVERS

It is a principle of law well established that an automobile is not inherently a dangerous instrumentality. It is not the ferocity of autos that is to be feared, but the ferocity of those who drive them.   *Superior Court of New Jersey*

WE DON'T AGREE

There will never be universal peace as long as one man raises chickens and another raises a garden.

Arcadia (Wisconsin) News-Leader

COST OF WANTING

Instead of dodging the issue of the high cost of food, let's face it squarely: Our major trouble is the high cost of wanting.

Ida Baily Allen

NOTHING MUCH TO DO

It was brought out at a recent Northwestern University psychology class that during an average housewife's lifetime she performs these tasks: Cooks 35,000 meals, makes from 10,000 to 40,000 beds, vacuums a rug a mile long and a tenth of a mile wide and cleans 7,000 plumbing fixtures. If you don't believe that, just try to figure it out for yourself.

Mickey McCarty, Indianapolis News

SATISFIED

A man may be disconsolate with everything—God, country, wife, art—but he is never discontented with the amount of sense he has. It is always enough.   *Ben Hecht*

AMERICAN CAPITALISM

While the U. S. economic system carries the label of "capitalism" it differs sharply from the static and "class-conscious" capitalism of the Old World. It is a new kind of capitalism—a capitalism that benefits everybody, not just the capitalists. . . . Almost everyone in America has had a share in developing and operating it.   *Paul G. Hoffman*

EXAMPLE

No man is so insignificant as to be sure his example can do no harm to others.

PECULIAR

A foreigner once commented: "You Americans are strange people. You devote one day out of the year to your mothers and an entire week to pickles." *Medford (Wisconsin) Star News*

IT TAKES THREE

It takes three persons to make a really good conversation; two of them here and the other far enough away so she can't overhear.   *Helen Meyer, Mason City (Iowa) Powerlite*

TOO LATE

Backward, turn backward, O Time in thy flight—I've just got a wise crack I needed last night.

AND GRAVY?

Sign in a Milwaukee restaurant window: "T-bone, 25¢." Then you get close enough to read the fine print: "With Meat, $4.00."

WHO SAID SO?

"The younger generation no longer respects its elders; it tyrannizes its teachers; fails to rise when older people enter the room, and has atrocious manners."

These are the words of a wise old man who lived over 2,000 years ago—Socrates, by name.

GETTING THERE QUICKLY

If you get up earlier in the morning than your neighbor, and work harder and scheme more and stick closer to your job, and stay up later planning how to make more money than your neighbor, and burn the midnight oil planning how to get ahead of him while he's snoozing, not only will you leave more money when you die than he will, but you will leave it much sooner.

GOOD ADVICE

Advice to speakers: In the old farmer's words, "When you're thru pumpin', let go the handle."   *Horizons*

CONFUSION

One Hollywood child explained to another: "I have 4 daddies by my 1st mama, and 3 mamas by my fourth daddy."
                              Automotive Dealer News

IS THAT CLEAR?

A self-styled labor reformer was watching a trench being dug with modern methods. He said to the superintendent, "This machine has taken jobs from scores of men. Why don't you junk it and put a hundred men in that ditch with shovels?"

The superintendent snorted, "Better still, why not put a thousand men in there with teaspoons?"
          Magic Circle, Perfect Circle Piston Ring Co.

THE BATTLE OF BLENHEIM

"And everybody praised the Duke
  Who this great fight did win."
"But what good came of it at last?"
  Quoth little Peterkin.
"Why that I cannot tell," said he,
"But 'twas a famous victory."

DOING THE WORK OF THE CHURCH

Dear Friend:

Our church membership	1400
Nonresident membership	75
Balance left to do the work	1325
Elderly folks who have done their share in the past	25
Balance left to do the work	1300
Sick and shut-in folks	25
Balance left to do the work	1275
Members who did not pledge	350

Balance left to do the work	925
Christmas and Easter members	300
Balance left to do the work	625
Members who are too tired and overworked	300
Balance left to do the work	325
Alibiers	200
Balance left to do the work	125
Members who are too busy somewhere else	123
Balance left to do the work	2

Just *you* and me—and brother *you'd* better get busy, for it's too much for me!   *Progress*

SAVING TIME

Salesman to prospect: "You can save yourself a rather dull 10 minutes by buying now before I get started on my sales talk."

BETTER: FROM MIDDLE BOTH WAYS

Lady reader, returning a library book: "Do you know, I simply couldn't put it down until I'd read it right thru to the very beginning."

IGNORANCE IS BLISS?

Becoming wiser today isn't an unmixed blessing. It causes a person to realize what a fool he was yesterday.

MANY TRY

Every nation finds it difficult to balance a budget at the end of a sword.   *Banking*

CHRISTIANS

Christians are like tea; their real strength comes out when they get into hot water.   *Clovis G. Chappell*

ONE THINKING

If you find 100 men in complete agreement, you can bet your bottom dollar that 99 of them are doing the agreeing, and one is doing the thinking.

Senate Democratic Leader Lyndon B. Johnson of Texas

SOMETHING TO DO

Compared with what we ought to be, we are only half awake, once declared Professor William James of Harvard. We are making use of only a small part of our physical and mental resources. Why do we work crossword puzzles? Is it because we wish to keep our minds busy? No, not that. It is because our minds want to be busy. The millions of tiny brain cells are crying for something to do. If we do not give them something to work at, they wear themselves out. As Longfellow once said:

> The millstone and the human heart
> Are turning ever 'round;
> If they have nothing else to grind
> They must themselves be ground.

SOUND MONEY

One thing we ought to keep sound as a dollar is the dollar.
Banking

CONGRESSIONAL SLOGAN

"Watch your step—the job you save may be your own!"

MIDDLE AGE

A man is middle-aged when he realizes he can't do as much work as he once could do . . . if he'd done it.
Marcelene Cox, Ladies' Home Journal

THE STORY OF MAN

When he is born, everybody thinks about his mother. When he marries, everybody thinks about the bride. When he dies, everybody thinks about his widow.

HAVE YOU GOT THE GOODS?

A lion met a tiger as they drank beside the pool. Said the tiger, "Tell me why you're roaring like a fool." "That's not foolish," said the lion, with a twinkle in his eyes; "they call me the king of the beasts because I advertise."

A rabbit heard them talking and ran home like a streak. He thought he'd try the lion's plan, but his roar was just a squeak.

A fox came to investigate—and had luncheon in the woods. So when you advertise, my friends, be sure you've got the goods!

Baltimore Ad Club Bulletin

HOW TO SELL POTATOES

Two farm wagons stood in a public market, both loaded with potatoes. A housewife stopped beside the first wagon and asked, "How much are your potatoes today?"

"A dollar and a quarter a bag," replied the farmer.

"Oh, my!" protested the woman. "That's pretty high, isn't it? I gave only a dollar last time."

"Taters have gone up," grunted the farmer, and turned aside.

At the next wagon, the housewife asked the same question, but Ma McGuire "knew her potatoes," as the saying goes. She spoke with enthusiasm. "These are especially fine white potatoes, ma'am. We raise only the kind with small eyes so there will be no waste in peeling. Then we sort 'em by sizes. In each bag you'll find a large size for boiling and cutting up, and a smaller size for baking. The baking size cooks quickly and uniformly, which means a big saving in gas.

"These potatoes are clean, too," the woman continued. "You could put a bag in the parlor without soiling your carpet—you don't pay for a lot of dirt. They're a good buy at $1.65. Shall I have them put in your car?"

The woman who thought the first farmer's potatoes were too dear, bought two bags from Ma McGuire at a higher price. All of which proves that it is more important to establish a value than to quote a price.   *Sunshine Magazine*

VACATION

Little bank roll, here we part, let me hug you to my heart. All the year I've clung to you; I've been faithful, you've been true! Little bank roll, in a day, you and I will start away, to a good vacation spot—I'll come back, but you will not.

Harvard Lampoon

THE REAL TEST

A car dealer's ad: "Come on in, browse around. Kick the tires."

WORTH REMEMBERING

There's always free cheese in a mouse trap, but you never saw a happy mouse there. *Parts Pups, Genuine Parts Co.*

HIS REASON

A father of five was asked why he had so many children. "Because," he said, "we never wanted the youngest one to be spoiled!" *Pipe Dreams*

WE LIKE HIM, TOO

There's a chap at our meetings
for whom I rejoice;
Thru debates and discussions I
long for his voice.
Tho he'll rarely say more than
4 words in his turn,
He'll deliver them clearly: "I
move we adjourn."

Leonard K. Schiff, Maclean's

VALUABLE ASSET

Students in a psychology class at San Diego State College were asked to name their most valuable asset. Two wrote down intelligence, and both misspelled it.

New York Journal-American

WE DIDN'T BELIEVE IT

Write down your house number. Double it. Add five. Multiply by fifty. Add your age (don't cheat). Add the number of days in the year. Subtract 615.

In the result you will find that your house number is to the left and your age is to the right.

JUST DAY DREAMING?

It's not what you'd do with a fortune, if riches would be your lot, but what you are doing today with the spare time you've got. Perhaps you're busy dreaming of getting a million or two; but what good is this dreaming if you don't make it come true?

THRIFT

Save your pennies and the sales tax will take care of them.
Banking

MEMORIAL DAY

Memorial Day weekend will be celebrated as usual by patriotic societies and speeding motorists. Old graves will be decorated; new ones dug.   *Changing Times*

SOME CHINESE PROVERBS

We cannot always oblige, but we can always speak obligingly. Everyone sees life through his own pinhole. Have the tools ready; God will find thee work. No man is free who is not master of himself. Liberty under the law does not mean license to break the law. That is lost that is misused. Labor makes known the true worth of a man as fire brings the perfume out of incense. Who has not tasted what is bitter does not know what is sweet. Zeal without knowledge is a runaway horse.

SAVING

About $10,000 is required to create each new job and we have to find jobs for about a million new workers each year. In other words, we must save about $10 billion a year (for new capital investment). People will not save that sum, unless they have a reasonable prospect of reward (profit) and the certainty of being permitted to enjoy the fruits of their frugality.
Harding College National Program Letter

NO INDISPENSABLE MAN

Sometime, when you're feeling important,
Sometime, when your ego's in bloom,
Sometime when you take it for granted,
You're the best qualified in the room,
Sometime when you feel that your going,
Would leave an unfillable hole,
Just follow this simple instruction,
And see how it humbles your soul.

Take a bucket and fill it with water,
Put your hand in it, up to the wrist,
Pull it out, and the hole that's remaining,
Is a measure of how you'll be missed.
You may splash all you please when you enter,
You can stir up the water galore,
But stop, and you'll find in a minute,
That it looks quite the same as before.

The moral in this quaint example
Is do just the best that you can,
Be proud of yourself, but remember,
There is no indispensable man.
    Anonymous (based on an ancient French proverb)

OPPORTUNITY

Many a man of 60 looks like 50, acts like 40, feels like 30, and can see plenty of opportunity walking along the streets he overlooked at 20.   *Wooden Barrel*

MANY TRY IT

If you want to go thru life completely misunderstood, say exactly what you mean.   *S. J. Mann*

UNIMPORTANT

I'm always losing rubber bands, and breaking package strings. Oh, the horrible importance of unimportant things!

WHO GAVE YOU YOUR JOB?

The chances are you will answer with the name of the individual or business institution which placed you in your position.

The Chamber of Commerce of the United States says you also owe your job to men and women you have never met—investors who supplied the money to get your company started, or to help it expand.

Though most of us never think of it, to create jobs costs money, and the cost is going up every day. Currently, the cost of tools and equipment and other outlays necessary to set up a single industrial job is about $15,000.

Census estimates are that the present work force of more than 70 million persons will increase to about 87 million in 1970, so that we will need to create more than a million new jobs every year just to keep pace. That adds up to better than $15 billion annually, most of it to come from investors.

In addition, new investment is needed to create jobs for employees in "declining industries," such as buggy whip makers of yesterday.

Investment money also pays for new tools and equipment for your present job, helps to increase your output. This means working easier, not harder or longer. And it is the only way to raise wages without creating price increases.

There is no point in merely recutting the same size pie, the Chamber points out. The trick is to make the pie bigger so that everybody gets more, nobody loses.

And so investors pretty much hold the key to America's future.   *Sunshine Magazine*

INDEX